How to Improve Your Mind

Scientific Methods for Managing Your Thinking & Emotions

RAVEEN HANWELLA

MBBS, MD (Psych), FRCPsych, FSLCPsych, FCCP
Professor in Psychiatry
Department of Psychiatry
Faculty of Medicine
University of Colombo

How to Improve Your Mind
Raveen Hanwella

© Raveen Hanwella 2014

First Edition July 2014
Revised Edition December 2014

Published by:
Kumaran Book House
39, 36th Lane, Colombo 06, Tel.: 112364550, 113097608
E-mail: kumbhlk@gmail.com

3, Meigai Vinayagar Street, Kumaran Colony, Vadapalani, Chennai 600 026
Tel.: 2362 2680

Printed by:
Kumaran Press Private Limited
39, 36th Lane, Colombo 06, Tel.: 112364550, 113097608,
E-mail: kumbhlk@gmail.com

Cover design by Raveen Hanwella

Contents

Foreword

Raveen Hanwella MBBS (Col), MD (Psy), FRCPsych, FSLCPsych, FCCP, Professor in Psychiatry in the 144 year old Colombo Medical School, was certified as a fully-fledged consultant psychiatrist in 1993, when he was barely 30 years old. Let me come right out and declare that Raveen is a psychiatrist who has matured precociously. When a professional with his credentials and experience writes a book which promises to tell you how to improve your mind, even I, his erstwhile physiology teacher now going on 82, feel compelled to look and see what he has to say. For goodness knows that my mind needs improvement; a fortiori, less senile and flexible minds than mine.

To fulfil his promise Professor Raveen offers guidance in separate chapters on coping with stress, managing our emotions, dealing with depression, pursuing happiness, obeying authority, thinking critically, and looking after our brains. The last chapter appropriately offers guidance on facing the ultimate reality of death.

The light he shines for us is the power of the human mind, concerning the disorders of which he has specialised modern knowledge. Remember it is with the mind - that is, the set of operations of the brain - that humankind has endeavoured to comprehend the mysteries of this world, including the weird behaviour of subatomic particles, by means of quantum theory. We have it on the authority of Nobel Prize winning theoretical physicist Richard Feynman however, that 'nobody understands quantum mechanics.' Even so on the basis of useful results obtained by the application of the scientific method, of hypothesis, deduction, and experimentation, we accept quantum theory to be as true as anything we know. As with quantum theory, so we with the theory of mind. Prof Raveen claims that the guidance he offers has been validated by scientific method.

In my youth, I turned to philosopher Bertrand Russell's book The Conquest of Happiness, published in 1930, in the hopes of improving my mind. But modern psychiatry is more reliable than old philosophy. So in my old age, I turn to psychiatrist Raveen Hanwella's How to Improve Your Mind for guidance. So should you, if you are sane.

Prof Carlo Fonseka
Emeritus Professor of Physiology
Faculty of Medicine
University of Colombo
Sri Lanka
2014

Introduction

Good mental health is the absence of mental illness. That would be similar to saying that good physical health is the absence of physical illness. Most people, especially the young, do not have any physical illness but are not physically fit. The person who can do 100 push-ups is physically fitter than one who cannot do any.

Physical health is relatively easy to measure. We can time how fast one can run 100 meters, or measure the maximum weight a person can lift. To measure mental health is not that easy and the lack of mental health is not obvious either. But good mental health is as important as, or even more important than, physical health, for our well-being.

Book catalogues have many books on how to increase physical fitness, but few on improving mental health. I have practised psychiatry for over two decades and seen most of the mental illnesses described in textbooks. I have talked to many people who, though not mentally ill, lead unhappy lives, and cause misery to those close to them. These individuals suffer from poor mental health. I cannot help these persons with medicines. However, I know techniques and principles of improving mental health derived from quality research. The general public does not have easy access to this knowledge. This book is my attempt to fill this void.

Raveen Hanwella

Chapter 1

Stress and Coping with Stress

Three persons came to me for help recently. The first was a businessman. He was wealthy and successful but could not sleep. "Doctor," he said, "if I don't take quarter of a bottle of whiskey and 10 sleeping tablets I can't sleep, and even after that when I get up I don't feel as if I have had good sleep". The second was a housewife. She had three children and her husband works abroad. She was referred to me by a neurologist colleague. She had a persistent headache for which no cause could be found. She said, "I have this headache that gets worse in the evenings. I get irritable especially with the children who are difficult to manage. I am worried as I have now started hitting them." The third was an A level student. She said she has lost her memory. "I keep looking at the books for hours but nothing goes in."

These people have a problem in common. They are all suffering from stress. What is stress? The word stress is derived from the Latin word *stringere* meaning 'to draw tight'. The term was originally used in physics to define forces that act on an object. In biology, stress is defined as the response of an organism to environmental change. Sometimes the word stress is used to identify the factors that cause stress. But it is more accurate to call these factors stressors.

Human beings, when stressed, react in a predictable manner physiologically. The physiologist Walter Bradford Cannon first described this in 1932 as the 'fight or flight' response. He theorised that animals react to a threat by

1

increased activity of their sympathetic nervous system. The sympathetic nervous system is part of the autonomic nervous system. The autonomic nervous system regulates the function of our internal organs such as the heart, stomach, and intestines. Increased activity of the sympathetic nervous system sends the body into 'battle stations'. The blood pressure rises increasing circulation of blood to the muscles. However, blood to organs that are not essential for action such as the digestive tract is reduced. Other changes include, an increase in the rate of breathing to bring more oxygen to the body tissues, increase in muscle tension to provide the body with extra strength and speed, dilatation of the pupils to increase the field of vision, speeding up of blood clotting to prevent bleeding in case of injury, and increased perspiration to prevent overheating of the body.

The word stress was coined later by a Hungarian born Canadian doctor Hans Selye. He injected mice with irritating substances, and discovered that whatever the substance the reaction of the mice was similar. He also observed that people with different diseases showed similar symptoms that he thought was due to the effect of a noxious agent he called stress. He went on to note that stress was stressful whether the news was good or bad. He called stress due to negative events distress and stress due to positive events eustress.

In 1967, two psychiatrists Thomas Holmes and Richard Rahe examined the medical records of 5000 patients to look for a connection between stressors and illness. The patients were asked to rate a list of 43 life events and indicate how much stress it caused them. The findings were published as the 'Social Readjustment Rating Scale' (SRRS), now more commonly known as the Holmes and Rahe Stress Scale.

In their scale, death of a spouse scores the maximum of 100. Even happy events such as marriage and Christmas score 50 and 12 respectively. If a person scores more than 300 points within one year, there is high risk of illness whereas those scoring between 150 and 299 have a moderate risk of illness.

Is stress always bad? The answer is no. All human beings have to face stressors in their daily lives. The normal response to stressors is adaptive and helps us face the challenges of life successfully. More than 100 years ago two Scottish psychologists, Yerkes and Dodson, discovered a simple but important law.

They showed that, if a person is subjected to stressors, the performance initially increases, but only up to a point. Beyond this point, the person becomes overwhelmed by stress and performance drops. This inverted 'U' is known as the Yerkes-Dodson Law. In simple terms, a little stress is good for you, but too much stress is bad. If we don't have any stressors in our lives, we will not achieve much in life and become a bunch of lotus eaters. Animals, especially the big cats living in the zoo, have a shorter life span than in the wild. They have plenty of food and don't need to hunt, but the daily trials of living which toughen their bodies are absent. On the other hand, if we have too many stressors in our lives, we become exhausted and, if the stressors are extreme, we give up.

Martin Seligman, a psychologist, showed this experimentally. He gave electric shocks to two groups of dogs (animal lovers, please note that these shocks were not painful, just uncomfortable). In the first group, the dogs could escape the shocks; in the second group, they could not escape the shocks. After some time, the second group of dogs became apathetic and did not even move when shocked. He called this state 'learned helplessness'. We see this state in humans too. People facing repeated and severe stressors simply give up on life and make no attempt to leave stressful situations even if they can.

The ideal is to have just the right amount of stress so that we have peak performance levels – the top of the inverted U.

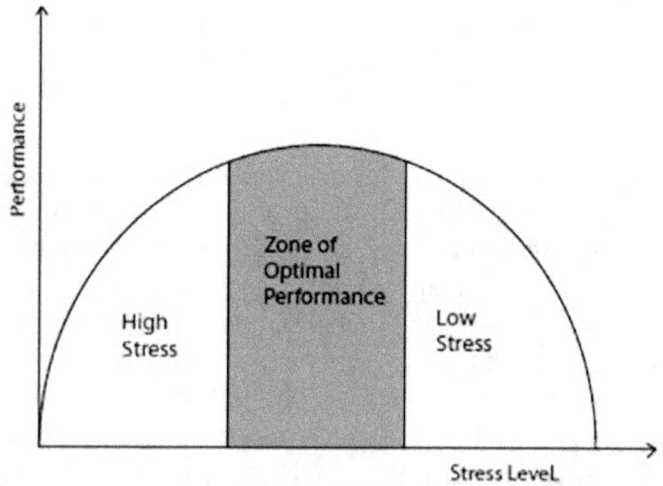

Fig. 1. Performance and stress levels

How do we achieve this? To an extent, this depends on our personality. We know people who thrive in difficult situations. They can do a hundred different things, all at the same time, but never get fazed. If you are not one of those lucky individuals can you become one? The answer is both yes and no. You can learn to cope better with stress. Perhaps you will not achieve the equanimity of those born immune to stress but certainly, you can learn to handle stress better than you do now.

Causes of Stress

There are many causes of stress, but all of these can be classified into just four groups.

Loss

The first category is loss. When we lose a person we love, there is grief and mourning. Loss is not confined to people but includes material things, the most obvious being money. It can mean other non-material forms of loss as well. For example, if a person loses his or her job, in addition to the financial loss, there is loss of status and dignity. If there were charges of impropriety, there is loss of honour and reputation. Sometimes these losses are more devastating than material loss. There are other subtle forms of loss such as loss of hope and aspirations. What you hoped for and expected to happen may be taken away from you. If these losses are sudden and unexpected, the effect is more overwhelming. This can lead to a state of hopelessness, which is a strong risk factor for suicide

Role change

The second category is role change. During life, we play many roles. At different times, or sometimes at the same time, we are required to play the role of father, mother, husband, wife, teacher, mentor, employer, etc. These roles cast certain responsibilities on and require from us, expenditure of thought and effort. For example, when a person gets married, he or she becomes a husband or wife and is required to take on new responsibilities. Even though marriage is usually a happy event, it is a source of great stress, especially with the drama and expense that goes into a 'traditional' Sri Lankan wedding. Therefore, role changes make demands and challenge the human psyche and lead to stress.

Conflict or dilemmas

The third cause of stress is conflict or dilemmas. By conflict, I do not mean physical battles or wars, but conflicts of the mind. A dilemma is a situation where a person is required to choose between two alternatives. For example, a person may be required to choose between two job offers or, between two partners. If one choice is clearly better than the other, there is no dilemma and hence no stress, but if the choice is not clear, and one is not clearly better than the other, it leads to a dilemma which results in mental conflict and stress. The degree of stress is relative to how crucial the choice is for that person's life.

Human relationships

The last cause of stress is the commonest, and that is human relationships. I am sure we all know this. We, humans, are social animals and need to live in communities. We need help from other human beings to live happy and fruitful lives. Relationships are a source of strength and joy, but can also cause great distress and unhappiness. Wars have been fought, and great leaders have fallen due to problems with other human beings. Paris, the Prince of Troy from ancient times, and King Edward the VIII from modern times are such examples. People who self-harm commonly cite relationship problems, either with their parents or partners as the cause. As we go through life we need other human beings but they can also be sources of pain.

Reducing Stress

Dr Herbert Benson is an American cardiologist and founder of the Mind/Body Institute at the Massachusetts General

Hospital in Boston. Over three decades, he has researched the connection between the mind and the body. In the best-selling book, *The Relaxation Response published* in 1975, he theorised that there is an opposite response to the stress response which he called the relaxation response. The relaxation response causes a reduction in the activity of the sympathetic system reducing heart rate, blood pressure, rate of breathing and rate of metabolism. Usually, this response is involuntary but Dr. Benson has demonstrated that this could be induced voluntarily with techniques derived from traditional systems of meditation.

In 1968 practitioners of Transcendental Meditation (TM) were brought into a lab at Harvard Medical School. TM was developed by Maharishi Mahesh Yogi, who achieved fame as the guru to the Beatles. TM was immensely popular in the 70's and 80's. The TM practitioners were volunteers aged 17 to 41 years and most had two to three years of experience in meditation.

These experiments showed that during meditation the body entered a state of reduced metabolism called hypometabolism. Hypometabolic states are not common and occur in sleep and hibernation. In this state, the metabolic rate is lower than when you sit quietly in a chair. The changes brought about by meditation are different to that of sleep. Though oxygen consumption is lowered in both conditions, there are differences. In sleep, the oxygen consumption decreases gradually by about 8% over three to four hours. In TM, there was a 20% reduction within three minutes. This reduction is remarkable and cannot be brought about voluntarily by any other means.

There were also changes in the EEG (electroencephalograph which is an electrical recording of brain waves). Increase of alpha waves and slower theta

7

brain waves (deep meditation) are seen during meditation but are not common in sleep. Other brain wave changes associated with rapid eye movement sleep (REM) the stage of sleep during which we dream, do not occur in meditation. Meditation is, therefore, different to sleep. It cannot be substituted for sleep.

Another change noted during meditation was the drop in lactate levels. Lactate is produced in our muscles during exercise. When there is a lack of oxygen, as during strenuous exercise, the body produces more lactate. Blood lactate levels fall rapidly within the first ten minutes of meditation and remain low during the period of meditation. Experiments show that people who are prone to anxiety develop panic attacks when injected with a solution of lactate suggesting that lactate plays a role in producing the signs of stress.

Interestingly, the blood pressure did not change with TM meditation. The average blood pressure of the TM volunteers was low and remained low during meditation. Perhaps they had acquired this lowered blood pressure through the practice of meditation.

The physiological changes that accompanied TM were opposite to that of the fight or flight response and Dr Bensons named it, the Relaxation Response. He also showed that these changes were not unique to TM and could be elicited by other types of meditation and techniques used in relaxation. Autogenic Training, Progressive Muscular Relaxation, Hypnosis with suggested relaxation are some of these techniques.

The German neurologist Dr H.H. Shultz devised Autogenic Training. It is a therapy based on six mental exercises. A person can shift voluntarily to a less stressful state of mind by practicing these exercises.

Edmund Jacobson, an American physician, developed **Progressive Muscular Relaxation** in the early 1920s. It is a technique for learning to monitor and relax the voluntary skeletal muscles (the muscles over which you have conscious control) of the body. Dr Jacobson theorised that anxiety neurosis was caused or aggravated by muscular tension and that reducing muscular tension by relaxation would produce the opposite physiological state. Since its inception, progressive muscular relaxation has been used for anxiety management and also to help induce hypnosis.

Given below are the basic steps in progressive muscular relaxation.

Wear loose comfortable clothes and take off any footwear. Find a quiet place and a comfortable chair (ideally not a bed as the purpose is to relax and not to sleep). Take five deep, slow breaths before you begin.

The muscles are relaxed in groups starting from the muscles of the face. It is not easy for a person to just relax his muscles. Jacobson found that it is easier if the person is asked to first tense the muscle and then relax, noting the difference between tension and relaxation.

Start by contracting the muscles of your scalp by raising your eyebrows. Hold for about 5 seconds and then let your eyebrows go to resting position. Next contract the muscles around your eyes by squinting, hold for 5 seconds and then let them gradually relax. Next contract the muscles of your face by tightly clenching your jaws, hold for 5 seconds and let the jaw go slack. Continue this sequence for the rest of the muscle groups in your body, the neck, shoulders, chest, and abdomen.

Here is a list of the different muscle groups and how each of them could be tensed

Forehead – raise your eyebrows as far you can.

Eyes - close your eyes tightly

Mouth – clench your teeth tightly

Neck and shoulders – shrug your shoulder up to touch your ears

Chest – tighten by taking a deep breath

Abdomen – suck your stomach in

Buttocks – tighten by pulling your buttocks together

Arms (start with your right arm) – tighten your biceps by flexing your forearm towards your shoulder and tighten your forearm muscles by clenching your fist

Hand – clench your fist

Entire leg – squeeze thigh muscles

Lower leg and foot – tighten your calf muscles by pulling toes towards you

Foot – curl your toes downwards

After you have relaxed all the muscle groups separately, take a few slow and easy breaths and relax your whole body. Check each muscle group sequentially for any remaining tension and relax them again if necessary. Your whole body should be relaxed now. Enjoy your feeling of relaxation.

The entire session should take about 20 minutes. After some practice, the relaxation response will kick in more quickly.

Hypnosis is an artificially induced altered state of consciousness. It is characterised by increased suggestibility. In a hypnotic state, a subject can be made to lose sensation in particular body areas, lose the memory for certain events, levitate their hands or disregard pain. Subjects can also be induced to feel relaxed. Hypnotic states are usually induced by a form of progressive relaxation. Though no specific set of physiological changes have been noted to characterise the hypnotic state, if deep relaxation is suggested, the physiological changes match those of the relaxation response.

Dr. Benson describes four elements to help elicit the **Relaxation Response**. These are common to all forms of effective meditation. They can be used to devise a generic form of meditation without any religious connotations. The four basic elements are; a quiet environment, an object to dwell upon, a passive attitude, and a comfortable position.

A quiet environment

Choose a quiet, comfortable room where you are not likely to be disturbed.

A mental device

Use a constant stimulus such as a phrase, word or sound repeated silently or aloud to prevent the mind from drifting and getting distracted with day to day thoughts. These words or phrases could have a religious meaning, but this is not essential. A neutral word such as 'one' is less likely to be distracting. The eyes should be closed, and attention to the rhythm of breathing would help enhance relaxation.

A passive attitude

This is the most important factor in eliciting the Relaxation

Response. Attempt to empty the mind of distracting thoughts. Do not focus or concentrate on any thoughts that come to mind during this exercise but allow these thoughts to pass through, as it is not possible to have no thoughts at all.

A comfortable position

It should be a comfortable posture one could remain in for at least 20 minutes. Do not lie in bed as the purpose is not to sleep.

In 2010, four decades after the publication of his book, *The Relaxation Response*, Dr. Herbert Benson published a book titled *The Relaxation Revolution*. In it, he puts forward the view that mind-body science has now reached a stage where it can be offered as a major preventive and treatment option along with drugs and surgery for a number of medical problems.

In his book, he adds a second phase to the eliciting of the relaxation response. This is the phase that provides healing for a particular illness or discomfort in the body. In this second phase which he calls 'visualisation,' the person is asked to visualise a state of wellness from the past. If a person is unable to recall such a period, he is asked to imagine such a state of wellness. For example, if the problem is that of a backache, the person should imagine being able to move around freely without any discomfort or pain. These dynamic images should be held in the mind for a period of 8 to 10 minutes.

This two stage exercise is called the Benson-Henry Protocol after its founders. Is there any scientific proof of its effectiveness? As proof, Dr. Benson cites a remarkable study done at the Benson-Henry Institute for Mind Body

Medicine at Massachusetts General Hospital, a major teaching hospital of the Harvard Medical School. Human beings have around 22,000 genes. All these genes are not active at the same time. They can be turned off or on. The number of genes that are turned on at any one time is termed "gene expression". By using a sophisticated new technology called microarray analysis the activity of all 22,000 genes can be checked, and the genes that are turned on identified individually.

The genes that are important in mediating the stress response are now known. For example, there are genes that control aging, the inflammatory response, and release of destructive oxygen molecules called free radicals. In this study, the gene expression of a group of people experienced in meditation was compared to a group inexperienced in such activity. The study showed that genes important in stress mediation were expressed differently in the experienced meditation group compared to that of the inexperienced group. In the second part of the study, the meditation inexperienced group was given eight weeks of training in eliciting the relaxation response and their gene expression retested. Remarkably it was found that even after this short period of testing, the gene expression of 400 odd genes in the group has become similar to the experienced group. In other words regularly eliciting the Relaxation Response can make fundamental changes in our body, down to the level of switching genes off or on.

Coping with stress

I will now discuss some ways of coping with stress. I said, if you remember, there were four basic causes of stress: loss, role change, conflict or dilemmas and human relationships.

Loss

Let us first look at how to cope with loss. By loss, we mean all types of loss: human beings, our health, money, relationships and others. Loss is inevitable, and all of us, at some point in our lives, would face losses. One way of coping with loss is to prepare for loss before it happens. A prudent individual would build up adequate financial reserves to prepare for monetary loss and sudden necessities. Similarly, we should try to build a reservoir of friends who would support us during difficult times. Friendships cannot be made overnight. It takes time and work to cultivate reliable friends.

We should not be too attached to a few individuals in our lives. Here, I am not advocating a prescription of detachment. Emotionally intense over-involvement with another is mentally unhealthy for both. The loss of one would lead to a collapse of the other.

The loss of a job or vocation is another loss. Again it is important to develop a wide range of abilities so that if we are unfortunate enough to lose our vocation we can divert to another occupation. This principle applies to our health as well. If we, through healthy eating and regular exercise, build a reservoir of good health we would fall sick less often, and even if we did, the impact would be less and the recovery faster.

Another important aspect of coping with loss is to 'let go.' Some ruminate endlessly about what is lost and remain miserable for the rest of their lives. They fail to appreciate that for most human beings, even after the greatest of losses, good things still remain. A person may grieve for years the loss of a loved one and reject the love and care of the people around him. Some not only grieve but feel angry about perceived or actual harm done by others that led to the loss.

Shakespeare's play Hamlet is a good example of the inability of people to move on, leading to further tragedy and loss. Hamlet's father is killed by his uncle, who then marries Hamlet's mother and becomes king. Hamlet broods over this outrage and plots his revenge. In the end, his uncle is killed and with him several others who were innocent of wrong doing. This includes Ophelia, the girl who falls in love with Hamlet and commits suicide when her love is rejected. The inability of Hamlet to move on caused loss and grief to many others.

Bereavement

All that lives must die, Passing through nature to eternity.
William Shakespeare, Hamlet, Act I, Scene 2

The death of a loved one is a special loss and leads to mourning or bereavement. How do we cope with or help others to cope with bereavement?

Elizabeth Kübler-Ross was a Swiss-American Psychiatrist who made the study of terminally ill patients her life work. In her book *Death and Dying* published in 1969, she described five stages that people go through when faced with the prospect of dying. Though she based her theory on observation of dying patients, later she expanded it to include bereavement.

The stages know by the acronym DABDA are, denial, anger, bargaining, depression, and acceptance.

15

In denial, people are in shock and may appear to act as if nothing has happened. This may surprise relatives who may be critical of the person for not mourning, but this is a protective mechanism and help people attend to practical aspects such the funeral arrangements.

In the stage of anger, people become angry with themselves and others, especially those close to them. They may also become angry with health care personnel who last treated the dead person. The bereaved person will become difficult to care for during this period. It is important to remain detached and non-judgemental during this stage.

The stage of bargaining is more usual in terminal illness where the family and the person affected tries to negotiate (usually with a higher power) a longer period of life, by change of lifestyle.

In the stage of depression, the reality of the loss begins to sink in, and the person becomes withdrawn, avoids visitors and spends much of the time crying. They feel sadness, regret, fear, and uncertainty. These emotions are normal during this stage and show that the person has begun to accept the reality of the situation.

In the last stage of acceptance, individuals come to accept the death of their loved one as well as their own mortality. The mood is calm and stable.

The process of normal bereavement usually lasts up to six months but may become reactivated during anniversaries of the death.

The work of Kübler-Ross helps us to understand the behaviour of people in bereavement. People can be helped to progress from one stage to another, at the appropriate time, rather than getting stuck in one or moving around from one unresolved phase to another.

Colin Murray Parkes a psychiatrist whose specialty is the study of bereavement divides bereavement into four phases: Numbness, pining, disorganisation and despair, and reorganisation. The first phase lasts from hours to days and is soon followed by the second phase. There are intense feelings of longing for the dead person accompanied by intense anxiety. These pangs of grief are transient and in-between, the person appears to function normally. There is a loss of appetite and weight and loss of concentration and short term memory. The bereaved person is often irritable and depressed. The third phase of disorganisation and despair follows. The person repeatedly goes over the events prior to death, looking to find a reason and even to correct it. Some report the voice of the dead person talking to them, usually when they are about to fall asleep. This is normal and not a sign of impending madness. A sense of the dead person being near at hand is also common. After some time, the intensity and frequency of grief reduce but may recur during anniversaries. The phases of grief do not go in a strict sequence and the bereaved person may oscillate between pining and despair several times before the final phase of reorganisation.

Most bereaved people do not need expert help for successful mourning. The traditional rituals of our culture are helpful in this regard. However, a few may get stuck in one of the stages and may need help to move on. This is more likely where, the death was sudden, unexpected, and untimely, the bereaved person was vulnerable (previous psychiatric disorder, unsupportive family) or where there was an abnormal attachment (ambivalent, dependent or insecure) to the deceased.

For example, people may become locked in the stage of denial. They may continue to act as if the deceased is still alive. They will retain the belongings of the dead person expecting them to come back anytime. This process is called mummification. The therapy for people in this stage is guided mourning where the person is helped to accept the reality of the loss. The bereaved are invited to bring photos or other objects linked with the lost person, talk about those items and write a 'diary' reminiscing about the deceased. The person could also be asked to visit the graveside. Sometimes the bereaved person gets stuck in the stage of depression and refuses to stop mourning. This is more

likely where the relationship with the deceased person was ambiguous. Therapy aims to help the person to stop grieving.

The most serious complications of bereavement are depression and risk of suicide. These are uncommon but if risk of suicide is high immediate intervention is needed. Many years ago Sigmund Freud pointed out the fundamental difference between what he called mourning (normal grief) and melancholia (depression). He said in grief, the world looks poor and empty, whereas, in depression, the person feels poor and empty. The second difference is that persons with depression experience profound loss of self-esteem, but the self-regard of persons engaged in a mourning process is not diminished. Therefore if a mourner feels worthless, and expresses a strong sense of general guilt and ideas of dying, it is time to seek professional help.

Sometimes people worry about anticipated loss or

18

possible losses that may occur in the future rather than an actual loss. Scientific studies shows that more than 90 percent of the problems we think might happen, never happen. In other words, 90 percent of the time we have worried unnecessarily. It is better to be an optimist rather than a pessimist. An optimist would be disappointed only 10 percent of the time!

Sir William Osler was a famous medical man. A founder of the Johns Hopkins School of Medicine he later became the Regius Professor of Medicine at Oxford. In 1913, he addressed the students of Yale University and gave profound advice on how to live a stress free life. In his lecture titled "A Way of Life," he recalled how he as a young medical student struggling to pass examinations, was inspired by the following words of Thomas Carlyle; "Our main business is not to see what lies dimly at a distance, but to do what lies clearly at hand." He advised them to live in day-tight compartments, like the water tight compartments of a great ocean liner, where at the touch of a button the bulkheads can be closed. He asked the students to "touch a button and shut out the past– the dead yesterdays. Touch another and shut off, the future- the unborn to-morrows. Then you are safe, safe for to-day."

A favourite poem of Sir William Osler, which he kept on his desk was, "Salutation to the Dawn" by the Indian poet Kalidasa. In it he says, *"For yesterday is but a dream, And tomorrow is only a vision, But today well lived makes every yesterday a dream of happiness, And every tomorrow a vision of hope."*

Role Change
Another significant cause of stress is role change. Examples

are taking up a new job, graduating from school or getting married. Even a happy role change can be stressful.

We humans and all organisms like to live in a state of equilibrium. The maintaining of equilibrium or balance of the internal environment of the body is called homeostasis. All our bodily mechanisms are geared towards maintaining homeostasis. If homeostasis cannot be maintained the body sickens and dies. This central tenet of biology was propounded by the physiologist Claude Bernard who went so far as to state,3999 "The fixity of the internal environment is the condition for free and independent existence." As much as the constancy of the internal environment is a necessary condition for healthy, and for human beings a happy, existence, there should be some constancy in the external environment as well.

Unlike the internal environment, we have less control over our external world, and again unlike the internal environment, living in unchanging surroundings or circumstances is inimical to healthy living. This may sound paradoxical at first. On one hand, to face change is to undergo stress but to live your life in a dull routine, day after day, is also unhealthy. The reality is that stress is caused by changes that are unexpected, changes that are extensive, and changes that we are not equipped to deal with.

This gives us a clue as to how to deal with change. True, some changes are wholly unexpected, but if you think carefully, most of these so- called unexpected changes could have been anticipated if not prevented. An example is that of a person who gets a myocardial infarction or 'heart attack'. It is a life changing, devastating experience for most people. In a minority of persons, it is truly unexpected but in most people, it could have been anticipated or even prevented. The family history

of heart problems, smoking those cigarettes ("it was just a few a day doctor"), the sedentary life style, the blood sugar that was not controlled, were all danger signs that were ignored. Therefore, an important way of dealing with stress, brought about by role change, is anticipation. We humans are far able to deal with changes that are anticipated than ones that are sprung upon us.

How do we anticipate change? After all, we cannot see into the future. Do we look at our horoscopes, or ask the astrologer? If we take time to reflect, the majority of life changes can be anticipated and plans made to deal with them. We all know that we have to start schooling at a certain age, study for a vocation, leave school, do a job, get married and start a family at different ages, and then if we live long enough, face the inevitable process of aging, retirement, and finally death. All these things can be planned for, and the unexpected turned into an expected event.

An extensive and major change in life roles is also a cause for stress. Sometimes this cannot be avoided. But, often with foresight and planning, role changes can be done in a stepwise manner avoiding sharp shifts in lifestyles. For example, if you need to change your career path, this could be done in stages allowing time to stabilise before moving on to the next stage.

Role changes that we are not equipped to deal with, cause severe stress. One of the most stressful jobs in the world is that of a being a member of a bomb disposable squad. Are people who take to this kind of job superior human beings immune to stress? A study done among members of the

British Bomb Disposal unit operating in Northern Ireland showed that this was not so. They were not superior beings but ordinary men. The difference was that they had received extensive training for their profession that enabled them to face their high risk job with equanimity. If we are well trained or we take the trouble to train ourselves well for the anticipated role changes of life, the level of stress experienced could be minimised.

Another factor that helps persons cope with stress is time. A person who is stressed needs a period of rest protected from other demands. This allows the system to rejuvenate and adjust so that he can deal better with the crisis. In relation to sickness, the sociologist Talcott Parsons called this period of required rest the Sick Role. The sick person is entitled to two rights; the sick person is not held responsible for his illness, and he is exempt from normal social duties. He did go on to say that the sick person has two obligations as well; that he should try to get well and seek help from a competent professional. A person in stress is commonly advised to take a rest, take time off or get a good night's sleep. As William Shakespeare said in his inimitable style,

"Sleep, that knits up the ravelled sleeve of care, the death of each day's life, sore labour's bath, balm of hurt minds, great nature's second course, chief nourisher in life's feast".

Another coping strategy is to change our attitude to the situation or map of the world. All of us see the world through filters. The first filter is our sensory organs. We can only comprehend what is within the range of our sensory systems. For example, our eyes can only see a certain range of light waves. We cannot perceive ultraviolet or infra-red light. Our ears can hear only limited range of sound waves. When we are young, we can hear the full range of a good quality stereo system which is usually 20 to 20,000 Hertz. As we grow older, this range narrows especially in the higher range. It is the same for our other sensory organs as well. Our sense of smell and our sense of taste get less with age to varying degrees.

The second set of filters is cognitive and lies within our brain. We filter the information we receive through, a set of values, attitudes, and views of the world. These filters are acquired over a lifetime and may be difficult to change. Filters are not inherently harmful. They are extremely useful. If not for filters our brains would be overwhelmed by the vast amount of information that we are bombarded with every moment, we are alive. But we have to remember that what we perceive may be distorted by the filters. A map is not the actual terrain but an accurate representation of the terrain. It has all the information we need to navigate from a point A to B. For a person to cope successfully when faced with a major change he needs to adjust his map of the world to the new reality. If a person suffers the death of a partner, then he or she has to learn to live without that person. The person's cognitive map of the world has to change. In addition to time, people would benefit greatly from the guidance given by others who have gone through a similar experience.

Dilemmas

The third category of stressors is dilemmas. Is there a scientific way of dealing with a dilemma? Before you attempt to solve a dilemma, think a moment. Do you have to choose between two alternatives or are there other choices? Maybe there is a third, a fourth or greater number of choices. When you are trapped in a dilemma don't try to choose immediately. Take time to think or discuss with friends or persons you trust. You will be able to think of more options. Once you know your choices clearly, is there a systematic way of choosing? Many years ago a psychologist called Goldfried suggested a method, now known as the problem solving method or problem solving therapy.

This method could also be used to resolve a dilemma. It has seven stages or steps. In the first stage, the problem is clearly identified. It is surprising how often people attempt to solve problems without first attempting to define and understand the problem clearly. You may well be attempting to solve the 'wrong' problem. This is often the case in problems involving children. A child may refuse to go to school. In our jargon, we call this condition school phobia or fear of going to school. So we assume that the problem must be in the school. Perhaps the child does not like the class teacher or maybe there is a bully who is making life unpleasant. Though these are common reasons, the real problem may lie elsewhere. Sometimes children refuse to go to school because of problems at home. For example, if the mother is not well, the child may fear that something would happen to her while he or she is away in school. What is needed in this situation is reassurance that the mother is being looked after and will get well soon.

Many years ago, I was told this story by a senior child psychiatrist. A child went to a Buddhist temple with her parents. Before entering the temple, she had to leave her slippers behind. On returning, she found her slippers missing. She was most distressed and to comfort her parents immediately bought her a pair of brand new slippers, exactly like the pair she had lost. To their surprise and perhaps annoyance she remained as distressed as before. I will leave you to work out the reason. The 'problem' is not sometimes 'the problem'. You have to look beyond the superficial issues otherwise, you will waste time trying to solve a non-issue.

Once you have clearly defined the problem, the second step is to think of possible solutions. It is important to brainstorm all possible solutions, however impractical they may seem at first. In the third step, rehearse each alternative solution until its implications are clear. In this step, you will be able to weed out the impractical solutions and select what is feasible. In a way you are thinking of the pros and cons of each solution, and working out the solution that has the least disadvantages and the most advantages.

The fourth step is to choose one solution based on your analysis in the previous step. This is an important step. Often people choose the first solution that springs to mind without a logical analysis, later to find that it does not work, or that there are insufficient resources to carry it out. The fifth step is to define and clearly think through all the steps needed. The sixth stage is to implement the solution. This may seem rather obvious, but people often hesitate to take action and procrastinate. They believe that if you do nothing the problem will go away. It often does not.

The seventh or last step, is to check the result. Is the outcome satisfactory? If yes, the problem is solved or the dilemma resolved. If not, another solution needs to be considered, and the problem solving steps gone through again. But that is simple you might say. Most effective therapies or strategies are that. They are simple.

Dealing with People

"Man is by nature a social animal; an individual who is unsocial naturally and not accidentally is either beneath our notice or more than human. Society is something that precedes the individual. Anyone who either cannot lead the common life or is so self-sufficient as not to need to, and therefore does not partake of society, is either a beast or a god. "

Aristotle, Politics

So said Aristotle. According to him, a person who likes to live in isolation and shun, or does not need the company of people, is either ill, inhuman, or a god.

Previously I stated there were four areas that cause stress for human beings. They are loss, change of role, dilemmas and finally people. In the majority of patients who come to me with depression or anxiety, at the root, lies a relationship problem. As Jean Paul Sartre said, in his play *No Exit*, "Hell is other people." We cannot live without other people, but most of our problems too are caused by other people.

Perhaps Aristotle is right. It is because man is a social animal (combined with his superior intelligence) that we have been able to dominate the world. Compared to some animals man is a puny creature but, by banding and working as a group, man has been able to overcome nature. Also, human beings spend a long period of time, relative to other animal species, being dependent on their parents.

Jacob Bronowski was a Polish scientist best remembered for his BBC television series *Ascent of Man*. The last chapter of the accompanying book is titled the *Long*

Childhood. He writes that relative to our life span, human beings remain dependent on other human beings for a long time. Humans learn more from their culture and environment than other animals whose behaviours are determined by genetic information pre-wired into their nervous system. This provides rich opportunity for human beings to overcome their nature and learn a range of new behaviours in a much shorter time scale than required by evolution.

Are human beings born as blank slates (tabula rasa) upon which anything may be written? *The Blank Slate: The Modern Denial of Human Nature* is a best-selling book by Steven Pinker, a Harvard psychologist. He argues against the tabula rasa model of the social sciences. He states that modern science has challenged three linked dogmas on human nature. The first is the blank slate, second the noble savage view, that people are born good and corrupted by society, and third, the ghost in the machine dogma which teaches that, each of us has a soul that makes our choices free from biology. However, Steven Pinker accepts that all human behaviour is not determined by biology

Does research help us to quantify the relative contributions of genes and the environment? The work done on the level of happiness of people show that of 50% is determined by genetics, 10 per cent by life circumstances and 40 per cent by their behaviour. I will discuss this in more detail in the chapter on happiness.

Man is a social animal, but he is also capable of violence against other human beings on a scale not seen among other animals. Around 37 million people were killed in the First World War and 60 million in the Second World War, a total of nearly 100 million people, five times the population of Sri Lanka. Sigmund Freud, writing soon

27

after the First World War postulated that humans have an innate drive towards destruction or a death wish. But Freud is not correct. The human instinct, as with other animals is survival. The rest is extra genetic or what we have learned during our long childhood and thereafter.

How can we manage our relationships better? We can find some answers in research findings on attachment, families, and emotions. In their bestselling book *Families and How to Survive Them*, published in 1983, Robin Skynner says, that though there is extensive research on dysfunctional families there is little work on healthy families. What makes healthy families healthy? Studies have identified several common characteristics of these super families. Most of this work has been done on middle class, white families in the United States and the UK, but probably the findings are valid for families the world over.

One such finding was that these families had an unusually positive attitude to life and other people. They enjoyed each other's company as well as others, and were friendly and reached out to other people. Did that mean that these families were unrealistically optimistic about other people? Not really. They had a more realistic view of the world than less healthy families. They understood that people could be good or bad. They accepted people as they are, but were willing to give the benefit of the doubt to people who initially did not behave nicely. They reached out to strangers in a positive manner, even though the initial response was not friendly. As a result, these families had a good relationship with their neighbours and were valued members of the communities in which they lived. This positive behaviour came naturally to these families. It was not a Dale Carnegie act where people gave out goodwill in the hope of getting it back. They had the confidence to not deliberately seek the approval of others.

The second important characteristic is, the love they have for each other. However, the love of these families is not the dependent, clingy sort of love found in less healthy families that leads to possessiveness and jealousy. It is a healthy love with closeness as well as distance. They have great affection for each other but don't need each other desperately. They can still enjoy themselves even when they are apart. As the Lebanese poet Khalil Gibran wrote so beautifully in his poem on marriage,

"...let there be spaces in your togetherness Love one
another, but make not a bond of love
Give your hearts, but not into each other's keeping. ...
stand together yet not too near together
For the pillars of the temple stand apart. "

Another characteristic of these families is how decisions are made within the family. The parents have clear authority in the family, but everyone in the family including the children are allowed to have their say. They are free to discuss the decisions and the parents'use of their authority, but when the occasion demands the children are expected to accept the authority of their parents without question. Because they are fully consulted, children in such families are prepared to accept the wishes of their parents even if they don't like it. So children can express how they feel but are not given too much power.

The fourth characteristic of a healthy family is that they manage to resolve conflicts as they arise. In these families, there are no chronic lingering resentments exploding into uncontrolled rage after a minor provocation, people know where they stand and there are no hidden agendas. They know when and why individuals in the family are happy or unhappy. After years of living in such an environment, members of such families become experts at understanding people and are able to accurately judge the feelings of others. In other words, they become more empathic.

Perhaps most of us do not come from such super families, but by studying their characteristics we can learn. As Bronowski said, most of our behaviour is not from our genes but by what we learn from other human beings after we are born. It is never too late for change.

Another characteristic of a healthy family is the ability to deal with change. As I mentioned before, change is a major cause of stress for people. But these families do not find change stressful. Not only do they cope with it but they seem to thrive on it. They actually enjoy change and find it exhilarating.

These families are sufficiently emotionally stable to request help from people when they need it. They are not embarrassed or threatened by having to do so. Research has noted that these families draw their support from three sources. The first is the rest of the family members. Because of the good relationship between family members this support is available all the time. The next is the community. As this kind of family usually has a good relationship with the community this support too is readily available. The third is a value system external to them.

The core system of beliefs gives a sense of meaning and purpose to life and goes beyond the personal welfare of the family. For most families, it comes from their religion. But a person need not be religious in the traditional sense. Even a non-religious person or atheist can derive solace from a system of values. The important thing is that this system should be based outside the person and be bigger than that person or family. It should be able to provide meaning and a purpose in the face of even devastating loss.

Victor Frankl was an Austrian psychiatrist who was imprisoned in a concentration camp by the Nazis. He lost almost his entire family in the camps. After the war, having survived the horrors of the concentration camp, he wrote *Man's Search for Meaning* about his experiences in the camp. He observed that the people who survived the camps had one thing in common. They all had a sense of meaning to their lives. In his book, Dr. Frankl says, "Those who have a 'why' to live for, can bear with almost any 'how'." He then went on to say, "Life is never made unbearable by circumstances, but only by lack of meaning and purpose." He was the founder of logotherapy, a therapy that tries to help people by guiding them to find a meaning to life.

Chapter 2

Managing Your Emotions

There was once a samurai warrior. In his lifetime he had killed many men in battle. One day, he started wondering whether he would go to heaven or hell. Looking for an answer, he went in search of a famous Zen master. After a long and arduous journey he came face to face with the master. He was not impressed with the Zen master because he looked like a simple peasant, and he doubted whether such a person could answer such a profound question. However having travelled so far he decided to ask him the question, "Is there a heaven and a hell and if so how could I get to heaven and avoid hell?" The Master asked, "Who are you?" The warrior replied, "I am the chief samurai warrior of Japan, and I work for the emperor." The Master laughed and said, "You are an ill-bred lout, go away and don't waste my time." The warrior was very angry and pulled out his sword to kill the master. "Stop," said the master, "that is hell." The warrior slowly sheathed his sword. "And that my son," said the master, "is heaven."

The warrior learnt an important lesson. Being angry is hell and ability to master your emotions is heaven. Heaven and hell are inside you and you can choose to spend your time in heaven or hell.

For many years it was thought that IQ or the intelligent quotient was the most important factor that determined success in life. However, the importance of mastering your emotions is now recognised as an equal or more important determiner of success.

Intelligence Quotient (IQ)

Alfred Binet, French lawyer and experimental psychologist is the father of the intelligence test. He was the first to devise a test able to measure higher mental functions such as abstract thinking and ability to generalise. In 1904, the French government appointed a commission to study the education of learning disabled children, and asked Binet to devise a test to differentiate between normal children and those with learning problems.

In 1905, with the psychiatrist Theodore Simon, he produced the Binet-Simon scale. He introduced the concept of mental age, the average ability of a child of a given chronological age. William Stern, a German psychologist, introduced the term Mental Quotient – the mental age of the child divided by the chronological age.

It was Lewis Terman of Stanford University who introduced the term IQ (Intelligence Quotient). He calculated the IQ by multiplying the mental quotient by 100. The test was renamed the Stanford-Binet Intelligence Test. It is one of the oldest intelligence tests currently in use.

In 1921, Terman used the Stanford Binet Test to start The Genetic Studies of Genius, today known as the Terman Study of the Gifted, to examine the development and characteristics of gifted children as they grow into adulthood. It is the oldest and longest running longitudinal study in the world.

Terman's wanted to disprove the theory that highly intelligent children were sickly, socially inadequate, and not well-rounded. He had a high opinion of precocious children (a view not shared by the American public at the time) and thought they should be given special schooling. He believed a decisive study would prove his view.

Terman did prove that gifted children were normal in health, though liable to be a bit more myopic than less gifted children (probably due to their spending more time on reading). The children in his study were called "Termites" and Terman carried on his study for 35 years and published his findings in five books. Initially, the study showed that gifted children became gifted adults. Some of Terman's subjects reached eminence in their fields (Over fifty men became college and university faculty members). However, the lives of the majority were ordinary. By his fourth volume Terman, perhaps somewhat sadly, noted that as adults his subjects pursued common occupations, "as humble as those of policeman, seaman, typist and filing clerk" and concluded, "At any rate, we have seen that intellect and achievement are far from perfectly correlated."

After his death, the study continued with new researchers (some were themselves "Termites") taking his place. Two such researchers, Howard Friedman and Leslie Martin wrote their findings in the book, *The Longevity Project: Surprising Discoveries for Health and Long Life from the Landmark Eight-Decade Study*. Some of these findings were expected, and some were not.

Here are some of these findings. Conscientious people live longer. They are less likely to take risks, have accidents, and smoke. Sociable and extroverted people have shorter lives than mild worriers, for similar reasons. Avoiding stress and leading an easy life does not increase life span but being engaged with meaningful work does. Divorce shortened the life of men more than women and being single was a greater disadvantage for men than for women.

The Marshmallow Test

In the 1960s Walter Mischel, a psychologist at Stanford University, did an interesting study. It was a test of ability to delay gratification in children at a preschool in Standford University. Most of the subjects were children of the university staff. The children were placed in a room empty of distractions. A marshmallow was placed on a table by the chair the child was seated on. The children were given the choice of either eating the marshmallow immediately or waiting 15 minutes till the researcher returned. Those who managed to wait without giving into temptation would be rewarded with another marshmallow.

Mischel observed that some children would "cover their eyes with their hands or turn around so that they can't see the tray, others start kicking the desk, or tug on their pigtails, or stroke the marshmallow as if it were a tiny stuffed animal, while others would simply eat the marshmallow as soon as the researchers left." Mischel tested around 600 children. A minority ate the marshmallow immediately. One third deferred gratification long enough to get the second marshmallow. Older children were more likely to delay gratification.

(Interested readers could search on YouTube to watch an amusing video of the Marshmallow Test.)

What was remarkable about the test was, the differences found between the children who delayed gratification, and those who did not, when they were studied 12 to 14years later as adolescents. Those who delayed gratification were, more socially able, personally effective, self-assertive with better coping skills and were still able to delay gratification. The children who could not resist temptation were socially shy, stubborn and indecisive and were more likely to become frustrated or stressed out and were still unable to postpone gratification.

In a second follow-up study two decades later, those who delayed gratification had significantly higher scores on their SAT scores. The third who waited had an average verbal score of 610 and math score of 652. Those who could not wait had scores of 524 and 528 respectively – a 210 point difference.

The ability to delay gratification is a powerful contributor to academic ability apart from IQ. What are the factors that are more important than IQ in determining successful living?

Emotional Intelligence (EQ)

Daniel Goleman is a psychologist, science journalist, and an author. In 1995, he published *Emotional Intelligence* that remained on the New York Times best-seller list for over 18 months. In it, he states that emotional intelligence (EQ) is more important than IQ and though IQ cannot be changed, EQ could be improved with training.

Peter Salovey, a psychologist, is now the President of Yale University. Along with John Mayer, he developed the concept of emotional intelligence. Salovey and Mayer defined emotional intelligence as "...the ability to monitor one's own and others' feelings and emotions, to discriminate among them and to use this information to guide one's thinking and actions." They classified EQ into five areas or domains:

The awareness of one's emotions

The ability to manage one's emotions

The ability to recognise emotions in others

The ability to regulate emotions in others

The ability to use emotions to motivate one's self

Let us look at each of these abilities in more detail. The ability to monitor our feelings is important for understanding ourselves. People who are not in touch with their feelings respond, without thinking, to their emotions. This could have disastrous consequences especially if the emotions are negative. For example, a driver who gets angry may afterwards drive dangerously without realising he is angry. Being self-aware of one's mood is technically known as metamood or mindfulness. Mindfulness therapy is now in vogue as a treatment for depression. Sigmund Freud referred to this state as a necessary quality in a therapist, where the therapist is able to monitor his emotions in response to what the patient is saying. To be self-aware, the people should be able to step back from themselves and observe their emotions dispassionately.

"Give me that man, That is not passions slave, and I will wear him, In my hearts core," said Hamlet in Shakespeare's play. The ability to master one's emotions has been appreciated as a virtue since the time of ancient Greece. The ability to keep one's emotions from extremes is indeed a useful ability and one that has been found to be independent of IQ. This does not imply an ability to show a bland perpetually smiling face, but the skill to keep strong unpleasant feelings in check and not allow them to completely displace all pleasant emotions.

One of the most destructive of such feelings is anger. Teaching people to control anger or anger management is an important component of psychological therapy. Psychologist Dolf Zillman, a pioneer in anger management research, advocates two main ways of dealing with anger.

The first is to take note of the thoughts that provoked the anger in the first place and reappraise the thoughts.

For example, if you get angry with a driver who cut in front of you, your first thought may be that he is doing it deliberately, or he is inconsiderate. But if you were to think that maybe he was distracted and did not really mean to cut in front of you, the anger would get less. Which assumption is actually true does not matter. The timing is important, if you allow the anger to escalate too much it would not be possible to think logically.

The second method is the traditional 'cooling off'. If, for example, you have got into an angry argument with a person, you should leave the situation temporarily. This will not work if after leaving the situation, you continue to ruminate on the issue that lead to the argument. If you were to do this, the anger would increase rather than decrease. During the cooling off period, it is best to distract yourself with different, more pleasant thoughts. Deep breathing, muscle relaxation and exercise also help.

The third attribute of EQ is the ability to recognise emotions in others. This is called social awareness. It is the capacity to understand the emotions, needs, and concerns of other people and pick up on emotional cues. Alexithymics are people who lack this capacity. Not only do they not understand their own feelings but they lack the capacity to know what people around them are feeling. It is difficult to understand how other people feel because we communicate mostly by nonverbal channels such as tone of voice, gestures and facial expressions rather than directly. People good at reading such nonverbal cues are more empathic than others. By focussing on others, making eye contact and paying careful attention to nonverbal cues we can improve this ability in ourselves.

The fourth EQ skill is the ability to manage emotions in others or the ability to manage relationships. This ability makes people popular, good leaders and excellent managers. This skill is in a way an integration of the previous three skills. People who are aware of their own feelings can control their feelings and recognise how others feel are better at managing relationships. Other skills which help people become good leaders and managers are organisational skills, the ability to network with people, negotiating skills or talent in arbitrating or mediating disputes, and social analysis, the ability to detect people's feelings, motives and concerns.

The fifth skill is the ability to use one's emotions to motivate one's self. World class athletes who have this skill can practice day in and day out to reach the top. The emotional quality of persistence and resolve in the face of setbacks, separate people who succeed in life from those who started life with a lot of advantages but failed.

Aristotle, in his *Nicomachean Ethics*, summed up emotional intelligence using anger as the example, in these words. "Anyone can become angry- that is easy. But to be angry with the right person, to the right degree, at the right time, for the right purpose, and in the right way – this is not easy".

Anyone can improve his or her EQ or emotional intelligence, provided the person is willing to put in the effort and time.

Chapter 3

Depression

I'll change my state with any wretch,
Thou canst from gaol or dunghill fetch;
My pain's past cure, another hell,
I may not in this torment dwell!
Now desperate I hate my life, Lend me a halter or a knife;
All my griefs to this are jolly,
Naught so damn'd as melancholy.

Robert Burton – Anatomy of Melancholy

Melancholy or melancholia is based on the old medical belief that disease was caused by an imbalance of the four humours (blood, phlegm, black and yellow bile) in the body. According to Hippocrates, melancholia was due to an excess of black bile hence the name which means black bile in ancient Greek — 'melas' black and 'khole', bile. In modern terminology, melancholia is the term used to describe a severe depression.

Robert Burton was a dean of divinity at Oxford and his *Anatomy of Melancholy* published in 1621 is a superb description of a pathological mental state. Burton himself suffered from melancholia. He learnt about mental illness from his own inner experiences and attributed his melancholy to his unhappy childhood and lack of parental affection. He was one of the first to highlight the importance of 'catharsis' as a primary healing factor and he emphasised the importance of a positive relationship in alleviating depression. "It is the best thing in the world to get a trusted friend to whom we may freely and sincerely pour out secrets". Burton ended his life by hanging himself in his rooms in Oxford

Symptoms of Depression

Moments of feeling sad, down or depressed is part of life. These arise in relation to day to day problems and resolve spontaneously in a short time. By depression, we do not mean such transient episodes of sadness. The medical use of the term means a syndrome or collection of symptoms that doctors call a depressive disorder. I will use the term depression in this sense.

Clinical depression is persistent, impairs day to day functioning, and includes a range of symptoms. There are different types of depression of which the most important is called, in psychiatric jargon, major depressive disorder (MDD). The main symptoms of MDD are a sad or low mood, loss of interest and pleasure in almost everything the person used to enjoy in the past. These include food, sex, work and being with family and friends. The symptoms are persistent and are present almost daily and should last for two weeks or more. There may also be accompanying physical symptoms such as disturbances in appetite (loss or increase in appetite), changes in weight (loss or increase in weight), sleep disturbance (trouble falling asleep, waking up in the middle of the night and not being able to go back to sleep, waking up early in the morning and feeling dreadful).

There may be other symptoms such as a feeling of restlessness (being unable to sit still, pacing or hand wringing), lethargy (slowness of speech and movements) or reduced energy. A feeling of tiredness and fatigue are also common. The tiredness is independent of physical exertion. Even little tasks require great effort and more time than before. Many persons with depression also report difficulty with concentration. They are easily distracted and complain of memory problems. In students, this may lead to a sharp fall in academic performance, and in the elderly, the memory loss may be sufficiently severe to be mistaken for early signs of dementia. This is termed pseudodementia.

Thoughts of death, feeling that life is not worth living, and ideas of suicide or even attempts of suicide are features of depression. These thoughts of dying may range from a passive wish not to be awakened in the morning, or die of an accident or illness, to contemplation of ways of committing suicide. Severely depressed persons may proceed to active planning for ending their life by collecting tablets or poisons and put their affairs in order by writing wills, paying off debts or giving away their possessions. Such behaviours may be warning signs to family members and friends of impending suicide. I remember the story told to me by another psychiatrist of a medical student who suddenly decided to give away his valuable wristwatch to his best friend. Fortunately his friend who also happened to be a medical student was alert enough to question him further to find that his friend was severely depressed and contemplating suicide. He was treated, and his life was saved.

It unnecessary to have all the symptoms described above to have a clinical depression. If you have five or more symptoms, persisting for several weeks that result in, impaired ability to take care of yourself or your family or cause significant problems in your working life then you probably have a major depressive disorder.

Types of depression

MDD is the main type of depression, but it is not the only type. In children, depression can present differently with severe recurrent outbursts of temper and physical and verbal aggression towards people and property, grossly out of proportion to the situation or provocation. These

43

outbursts occur around three or more times per week on average and in between the mood is irritable or angry most of the time. It is important to diagnose and treat this condition as otherwise, it would lead to serious disruption of school work. There is also a risk of progressing to adult type of depression in later years.

Another more severe form of depression is called psychotic depression. In this form, there is a distortion of thinking, in addition to the features described for MDD. Persons with such depression feel guilty and blame themselves for perceived wrongs. They may also feel that the depression was brought about because they have been bad or done a crime. Though not common it is important to identify this kind of depression as it needs treatment urgently and will not respond to psychotherapy.

Another form of depression is dysthymia. Symptoms are milder than in MDD. Symptoms are persistent and for definitive diagnosis should have lasted for more than two years in the case of adults and one year in children and adolescents. Though symptoms are less severe than for MDD, it is important to diagnosis this condition as it can seriously impair the enjoyment of life and productivity. These individuals are more likely to develop MDD in later life.

In some, depression is a part of another psychiatric disorder called bipolar disorder. Individuals with bipolar disorder, in addition to episodes of depression, also suffer from manic episodes. In manic episodes, the mood is elevated, expansive or irritable. There is increased activity, racing thoughts, feeling of excessive power (grandiosity), unrealistically high self-esteem and easy distractibility. Such individuals engage in activities with potentially damaging consequences such as excessive spending, abuse of drugs and alcohol and sexual excesses.

It is important to identify bipolar disorder as it is usually a life time affliction with serious negative consequences health wise and socially. The treatment is different and more complicated than for depression.

A new category of depression that has entered our books is Premenstrual Dysphoric Disorder. This is not a new entity and has been previously called by various names such as premenstrual syndrome. Recently it has been recognised as a separate type of depression. In this condition, the person becomes moody, irritable and anxious prior to menstruation. These symptoms resolve once menses start or shortly thereafter. To diagnose this condition, these changes should occur in most cycles for at least a year and should affect work and function significantly.

The causes of depression

In the past, depression was divided into two types; endogenous or biological depression and reactive depression. Endogenous depression is mainly due to biological or genetic factors and reactive depression due to adverse life circumstances. However, it is now recognised that depression in most cases is due to a combination of biological factors and problems in the environment.

Is depression inherited? First degree family members of individuals with depression have two to fourfold higher risk of developing the condition than the general population. There is no single gene that determines whether you will get depressed or not, but it is the inheritance of 'neurotic' personality traits that increase the vulnerability to depression.

How to know whether you are depressed?

If you feel you have the features of a depression described above, it is best to see a psychiatrist to confirm the diagnosis and start treatment. Given below is a standard questionnaire that you can use to determine your overall depression score. This questionnaire is called the Center for Epidemiologic Studies Depression Scale or CES-D for short.

Center for Epidemiologic Studies Depression Scale (CES-D)

Instructions: This set of questions is related to how you felt or behaved in the past one week. Using the scale below, please write the number that best describes how often you felt or behaved this way during the past one week.

0 – Rarely or none of the time (less than 1 day)

1 – Some or a little of the time (1-2 days)

2 – A moderate amount of the time (3-4 days)

3 – Most or all of the time (5-7 days)

1. I was bothered by things that usually don't bother me.

2. I did not feel like eating; my appetite was poor.

3. I felt that I could not shake off the blues even with help from my family or friends.

4. I felt that I was just as good as other people. (X)

5. I had trouble keeping my mind on what I was doing.

6. I felt depressed.

7. I felt that everything I did was an effort.

8. I felt hopeful about the future. (X)

9. I thought my life had been a failure.

10. I felt fearful.

11. My sleep was restless.

12. I was happy. (X)

13. I talked less than usual.

14. I felt lonely.

15. People were unfriendly.

16. I enjoyed life. (X)

17. I had crying spells.

18. I felt sad.

19. I felt that people disliked me.

20. I could not get "going."

How to calculate your score

Your scores on items marked with X should be reversed from 0 to a 3, 1 to 2, 2 to 1 and a 3 to 0. Now add your scores for all the 20 items. If your score is more than 16 you probably have a depression. The higher the score, the more severe the depression.

Radloff LS. The CES-D scale: a self-report depression scale for research in the general population. Applied Psychological Measurement. 1977;1:385-401.

The treatment of depression
Antidepressants

Until the 1950s, there were no effective medicines for treating depression. The first effective antidepressant developed was imipramine and after 60 years it is still in use. Though we now have a plethora of antidepressant drugs, none are more effective than imipramine.

Roland Kuhn was a Swiss psychiatrist who worked in the Muensterlingen Psychiatric Hospital. The hospital budget for the purchase of medicines was small, so Dr. Kuhn asked the drug manufacturing giant Ciba-Geigy in Basle whether they had any new drugs to try out on his patients with schizophrenia. The company sent him a chemical code named G22355 (later named imipramine). He used it on his patients with schizophrenia whose psychotic symptoms did not improve, but being a careful observer he noticed that some of them who also had depression improved. He then tried the drug on his depressed patients and within three weeks most of them were much better. The story goes that even then Geigy was not interested in the medication until one of its directors gave some to his depressed aunt who made a dramatic recovery. The company then decided to market the medication under the brand name Tofranil. The antidepressant era had begun.

Even though imipramine is a wonderful antidepressant it has some unpleasant side effects such as dry mouth, constipation, and blurred vision. It is toxic in overdose and can lead to abnormalities of rhythm in the heart and even cardiac arrest, not an ideal drug to leave in the hands of a depressed and suicidal patient. In the 1970's scientists working at the American drug company, Eli Lilly discovered fluoxetine, a new class of antidepressants called SSRIs (serotonin specific reuptake inhibitors). It was easy to take (one capsule a day), did not have the unpleasant side effects of imipramine and was much less toxic in overdose, and could be safely given to patients who were suicidal. It became one of the most successful drugs in history and at its peak reached sales of 3 billion dollars. Marketed under the name Prozac, it achieved the status of a cultural icon inspiring a book *Listening to Prozac* and even a film, *Prozac Nation*.

The prescription of antidepressants, especially in the US and other Western countries, has continued to rise and in the US is now only second to heart medication. In 2008 an article in the Scientific American, titled "The Medicated Americans," noted that nearly 10 percent of Americans were on antidepressants. Does it mean that the incidence of depression has increased over time? The answer is both yes and no.

The psychologist Martin Seligman summarised the results of a large scale study done in the US, "If you're born around World War II, the lifetime prevalence of depression is about 5%. If you were born starting in the 1960s, the lifetime prevalence is between 10 and 15%, and this is with lives incomplete." Seligman also noted that the age of onset of the first depressive episode has dropped. A generation or two ago the onset of depression occurred on average at age 34 or 35, but recent studies show the mean age for the first bout of depression to be at age of 14 years. Therefore, there is evidence that the prevalence of depression has increased but not as much as the number of prescriptions for depression.

Most of these prescriptions were not written by psychiatrists, but general practitioners and it would be reasonable to assume that the majority were not given for clinical depression. Doctors (at least in the US) have been quick to prescribe antidepressants for any complaint of feeling moody, sad, or being down without actually checking carefully whether they have the definite features of the disease called depression. They have used these medicines as a "happy pill" rather than as an antidepressant.

As mentioned before, clinical depression has very distinctive features that should be there almost every day and should have lasted for more than two weeks. Transient unhappiness due to life circumstances does not respond to antidepressant medication.

Currently, there are more than 30 different kinds of antidepressant medication. Each of them has different side effects. These are less severe than for the old tricyclic antidepressants like imipramine.

People starting antidepressant should note the following important fact. Unlike most medicines, antidepressants do not have an immediate effect. All antidepressant drugs currently in use, require two weeks or longer to act. Scientists are not sure of the reason for this delay. This may be due to the time taken for chemical changes in areas in the brain that play a role in emotion.

Unfortunately, the side effects of the antidepressant drugs occur almost immediately. Even the newer antidepressant drugs have side effects. For example, fluoxetine (Prozac) may cause irritation of the stomach, flatulence, and nausea. The person may also become more anxious and jumpy due to the stimulant effect on the nervous system. Fortunately, as the body adapts to the medicine with continued use, these side effects become less. However, because of the rapid onset of side effects patient starting on antidepressant medication may feel worse than before during the first three weeks of treatment.

Antidepressant drugs have had bad press in recent years. One concern has been that some types of antidepressant drugs increase ideas of suicide, especially in younger people. In response to these concerns, the US Food and Drug Administration has issued a black box warning for the use of antidepressants in children and young adults. Is this concern justified? A recent study analysed all the data from studies related to two popular antidepressants, fluoxetine, and venlafaxine. It found no increase in suicidal thoughts or behaviour in younger patients. Most reports of an increase in suicidal thoughts or acts while on antidepressants have been from Western countries and tied in with litigation. In contrast, studies have repeatedly demonstrated that, if used in proper dosage, for correctly diagnosed depression, antidepressants significantly reduce the risk of suicide.

Persons who think they may have a depressive disorder should confirm the diagnosis by consulting a doctor, before starting antidepressants. It is important that once started, medication should be continued for as long as recommended by the doctor.

Electroconvulsive therapy (ECT)

What are the other options available for treatment of depression? One is electroconvulsive therapy or ECT. In 1937, an Italian neurologist Ugo Cerletti thought that people who had epilepsy were less likely to have schizophrenia and if a fit could be artificially induced in persons with schizophrenia they would improve. Initially, he tried inducing fits with a chemical called metrazol, but the fits were severe and difficult to control. Cerletti knew that fits could be produced by passing an electric shock through the brain. This was more amenable to control than a chemical. His first patient was a vagrant from the central railway station in Rome. It is probable from the description given, that this person had schizophrenia. After several shock treatments, the patient made a remarkable recovery. Initially, ECT was mainly given for treatment of schizophrenia. Though some patients did recover, it was later found that ECT was more effective in treatment of depression. Even people with severe depression had quick and dramatic recoveries with ECT.

One Flew Over the Cuckoo's Nest was an Oscar winning American film starring Jack Nicholson that depicts the use of ECT. Though a brilliant film, it portrayed ECT in a negative light, where it was used for control and punishment rather than treatment. In the olden days, the fit was unmodified, and many patients suffered fractures of the spine due to violent seizures. Now patients are given a short-acting general anaesthetic and succinylcholine, a drug that paralyses the muscles prior to administration of ECT. After the patient is put to sleep, two electrodes are placed on the patient's head and an electrical impulse lasting a few seconds is set off. The patient is woken up soon afterward from the anaesthesia and usually suffers nothing worse than a headache and a short period of memory loss. In an otherwise fit person, ECT can be safely given as an outpatient procedure. Does ECT cause brain damage? Repeated testing of patients, some, who have had several hundred shock treatments in their lives, does not show any damage to the brain from ECT.

As I mentioned before, all antidepressants available in the market today take more than two weeks to show an effect. ECT is the only antidepressant treatment available currently that works faster than antidepressant medication. In a person with severe depression who has stopped eating and drinking, or in an elderly person where the side effects of antidepressants can be dangerous, ECT is lifesaving. The factors that prevent the more widespread use of ECT in the treatment of depression are public prejudice and the timidity of some clinicians. The respected Oxford Textbook of Psychiatry goes on to say "The safety of modern ECT is such that even the frailest and systemically ill elderly can be safely treated with ECT. We acknowledge no known absolute contraindication to ECT other than the lack of skill of the clinician".

Some time ago one of the doctors working in my unit asked a number of patients who had undergone ECT about their experience. The majority were highly positive and said though initially they were nervous, having undergone the therapy, they would not be afraid of going through treatment again and would recommend the treatment to anybody who needed it. Prof Max Fink in his book *Electroshock–Restoring the Mind* quotes a practising psychiatrist who had ECT for depression, "After the first treatment, I felt a blunting of the acute sadness of the depression. Whereas before treatment I became tearful with very little provocation and felt intensely sad out of all proportion to the stimulus. After one single treatment, I was no longer crushed by any chance sadness. The troublesome symptom of irritability also subsided early in the course of treatment." The psychiatrist then goes on to say, "I hope that this account will help to dispel the erroneous belief that ECT is a terrifying form of treatment crippling in its effects on the memory and in other ways. The technique is today so refined that the patient suffers a minimum of discomfort, and the therapeutic benefits are so great in those cases where it is indicated that it is a great pity to withhold it from mistaken ideas of kindness to the patient".

A word of caution here, ECT though an excellent treatment where it is indicated, is not a panacea for all psychiatric illnesses. It is effective for severe depression, some types of schizophrenia, bipolar illness and some medical conditions such as catatonia and Parkinson's disease. It is not effective, and should not be used for anxiety disorders such as obsessive-compulsive disorder, and acute attacks of anxiety (panic attacks) or in mild depressions brought on by life problems.

Psychotherapy for depression

There are two psychological therapies scientifically proven to be effective for depression. The first is cognitive behaviour therapy (CBT), and the second is interpersonal therapy (IPT). The older therapy is CBT and its two well-known pioneers are Aaron Beck and Albert Ellis. Albert Ellis was a psychologist who passed away in 2007 at the age of 94. Aaron Beck is a psychiatrist who at the time of writing is 92 and still working and writing.

Rational Emotive Therapy (RET)

Albert Ellis is the father of Rational Emotive Behaviour Therapy (REBT). REBT originally called Rational Emotive Therapy (RET) is a form of CBT. It is rooted in the ancient philosophical tradition of stoicism. The stoic Epictetus, in the first century A.D., wrote in the *Enchiridion*, "Men are disturbed not by things, but by the views which they take of them." William Shakespeare, writing many centuries later, rephrased this thought in Hamlet: "There's nothing good or bad, but thinking makes it so." In the book of Proverbs in the Old Testament of the Bible, it says, "For as he thinks within himself, so is he."

The basic premise of REBT (that it shares with CBT) is that it is what people believe about situations they face, not the situations themselves, which determines how they feel and behave. REBT states that a person's biology or inheritance may also determine how they think and behave, limiting a person's ability to change. Ellis called his model of REBT the ABC model. 'A' stands for activating event or adversity. It refers to the aspect of a situation that troubles a person most. It may be an actual event, an inference about an event, or an aspect of the event. This inference can be accurate or inaccurate. 'B' stands for beliefs. These can be rigid or flexible, extreme or non-extreme, general or specific. But more on that later. 'C' stands for consequences. These are the emotional, behavioural, and cognitive consequences of a person's beliefs about 'A'.

Let us see an example as to how this model works. A woman prone to depression meets an old friend on the street. The friend appears not to notice her and passes by. This activating event leads the women to infer that her friend deliberately ignored her. This inference leads to the belief that because the friend ignored her she must be unworthy as a friend and, therefore, also unworthy as a person. This belief leads to the emotional consequence of depression and perhaps the behavioural consequence of avoiding people in general.

Ellis argued that irrational beliefs lie at the heart of peoples' emotional problems which are brought on by life's adversities. Of these irrational beliefs, the most important are rigid beliefs in the form of musts, shoulds and have-to's.

In his book *The Essence of Rational Emotive Therapy* written in 1994, he listed some of these rigid beliefs or rules of life.

> It is a dire necessity for adults to be loved by significant others for almost everything they do.

> Certain acts are awful or wicked, and people who perform such acts should be severely damned.

> It is horrible when things are not the way we like them.

> Human misery is invariably externally caused and is forced on us by outside people and events.

If something is or may be dangerous or fearsome we should be terribly upset and endlessly obsess about it.

It is easier to avoid than to face life's difficulties and self-responsibilities.

We absolutely need something stronger or greater than ourselves on which to rely.

We should be thoroughly competent, intelligent, and achieving in all possible respects.

Because something once strongly affected our life, it should indefinitely affect it.

We must have certain and perfect control over things.

Human happiness can be achieved by inertia and inaction.

We have virtually no control over our emotions, and we cannot help feeling disturbed about things.

Looking at this list, most people would see that they have held one or more of these ideas even temporarily.

How do we go about changing our beliefs? According to REBT theory, change is possible at different levels. For example, if you feel anxious that somebody important in your life disapproves of you, you can feel better by altering your body chemistry by exercise, meditation, or medicines such as anxiolytics. You can also try to change the situation by avoiding the person. You can change the way you think about the situation by thinking that the person does not disapprove of you. But such strategies only helps a person feel better. To actually get better, as Ellis would put it, more fundamental changes have to occur in your core beliefs. This would help you face a range of difficult situations rather than one particular situation.

In the example above, rather than simply believing that disapproval might not occur, you must be able to accept that even when there is disapproval, it would not matter too much for your life. Thereby you change your core belief that approval is a necessity of life and that you must never receive disapproval. Or in other words, you must change the belief that to be happy in life you must always have the approval of other people.

Cognitive Behaviour Therapy (CBT)

Aaron Beck, Emeritus Professor of Psychiatry of the University of Pennsylvania is considered by many to be the father of cognitive behaviour therapy. Though Ellis accused Beck of borrowing his ideas, it is Beck who placed CBT on a firm scientific foundation by doing a number of studies comparing CBT with other therapies in the treatment of depression. The ideas are similar, but the jargon and the emphasis are somewhat dissimilar. Both Aaron Beck and Albert Ellis started life as psychoanalysts following the therapeutic tradition of Sigmund Freud. Both became dissatisfied with the results and slow pace of psychotherapy.

Classical psychoanalysis considers conscious thoughts as a disguised form of unconscious conflicts that lie at the heart of the problem. The patient's own explanations are considered as false rationalisations or defence mechanisms. According to Beck, this meant that the person's reasoning and judgements and practical solutions were not taken seriously but merely considered as pointing to deeper, concealed problems in the mind. He was also critical of behaviour of therapists and neuropsychiatrists.

Behaviour therapists, he said, in their eagerness to emulate the precision of physical science, reject data derived from man's reflections on his conscious experiences. They only consider useful behaviour that can be directly observed. Neuropsychiatrists inquire about a person's thoughts and feelings mainly to diagnose. Abnormal ideas and feeling states were thought of as manifestations of an underlying physical process or neurochemical abnormality. Such thinking said Beck, undermined a person's self-confidence and led patients to believe that they cannot help themselves. These therapies also devalue common sense and inhibit a person from using his own judgment in solving his problems.

Beck first developed his ideas on cognitive therapy in relation to depressive disorder. He noticed that people who were depressed had depressive, negative or pessimistic thoughts. This was no surprise because it was thought that the pervading low mood state gave rise to these thoughts. However, what was unusual was that after making an apparent recovery depressed people continued to have more depressive or negative thoughts than those without a history of depression. Based on these observations Beck speculated that it was the depressive and pessimistic thoughts that gave rise to depression rather than the other way around.

In psychoanalysis, patients are asked to express whatever thoughts come to their mind, no matter how trivial or unpleasant they may be. This is called free association and is one of the fundamental tools of psychoanalytic therapy. Beck, while doing psychoanalysis with his patients realised that in addition to the reported content of their thoughts they also had a parallel stream of thought of a self-critical nature. He also noted that these thoughts preceded an unpleasant emotional state. He called these thoughts negative automatic thoughts (NATS), negative because they are associated with unpleasant emotions, and automatic since they appear without a deliberate reasoning process. As a person becomes more depressed NATS become more frequent and intense and more rational thoughts are gradually crowded out.

How do negative automatic thoughts arise? Beck thought that the early life experiences of a person gave rise to certain core beliefs which in turn led to assumptions or rules about life. If these rules are dysfunctional, they give rise to negative automatic thoughts in the face of stressful life situations. These dysfunctional assumptions are somewhat similar to the rules of life described by Ellis.

Cognitive distortions

Here are some of the common dysfunctional assumptions or cognitive distortions that have been identified. The following list is from the book *Feeling Good* by David Burns.

1. All or nothing thinking

This refers to black and white thinking technically called dichotomous thinking. The person thinks in the absolute, with no allowances for shades of grey. For example, an otherwise bright student, who gets low marks in a particular subject, might think, "I am a total failure." People who indulge in this kind of thinking are always looking for perfection, never allowing for mistakes in their life. This thinking is unrealistic as the universe is rarely absolute. Such thinking will set you up for failure as you will not be able to live up to your exaggerated expectations.

2. Overgeneralisation

In this cognitive distortion, the person arrives at a general conclusion based on a single incident or a single piece of evidence. If something bad happens only once, you expect it to happen over and over again. A person may see a single, unpleasant event as part of a never-ending pattern of defeat. For example, a woman whose husband forgets her birthday may accuse him of not caring for her.

3. Filtering

Selecting the negative details and magnify them while filtering out all positive aspects of the situation. For example, a person receiving feedback about his work filters out all the positive comments and focuses on the suggestions for improvement and sees them as evidence of overall poor performance. The technical term for this is selective abstraction.

4. Disqualifying the positive

The person does not merely ignore positive experiences but transforms them into negative ones. An example is a person who responds to a compliment by saying, "it was nothing" who thinks that the other person was just trying to be nice and not sincere in his complements. This is an extremely destructive cognitive distortion.

5. Jumping to conclusions

Arbitrarily arriving at a negative conclusion that is not justified by the facts. We know what people feel or why they act in certain ways even when they do not express their thoughts. We are particularly able to determine what others feel about us. This distortion can take two forms. The first is 'mind reading'. For example, you may decide that someone is reacting negatively towards you without trying to find out if you are correct. The other variety is 'fortune telling'. For example, you may anticipate that things will turn out badly, and become convinced that your prediction is correct.

6. Magnification and Minimisation

Giving proportionally greater weight to a perceived failure, weakness or threat, or lesser weight to a perceived success, strength or opportunity. In other words, it is blowing things out of proportion or making mountains out of molehills or the opposite. An extreme form is catastrophizing, which is giving greater weight to the worst possible outcome, however unlikely, or experiencing a situation as unbearable or impossible when it is just uncomfortable.

7. Emotional reasoning

Taking emotions as evidence for the truth. For example, if I feel like an idiot I must be an idiot, or if I feel guilty I must have done something bad or, I feel hopeless, therefore, my problems are insolvable.

8. Should statements

Doing, or expecting others to do, what they morally should or ought to do irrespective of the situation. You try to motivate yourself with statements like, "I should do this" and "I should do that". Albert Ellis called this "musturbation". When such statements are directed at others and the others do not respond to your expectations it leads to anger and frustration.

9. Labelling and mislabelling

It is an extreme form of overgeneralisation where the person's actions are attributed to his character. In other words rather than assuming the behaviour to be accidental or extrinsic, you assign a label to someone or something that implies the character of that person or thing. For example, you think someone who made a bad first impression is a "bad character", in the absence of some more specific cause.

10. Personalisation

Seeing yourself as the cause of a negative event even when there is no justification for thinking so. For example, a mother whose son is not performing well in school thinks that she is a bad mother.

The above ten cognitive distortions are responsible for most depressive states. Study them well and learn to identify them in your life.

According to Beck's cognitive theory of depression, three levels of thinking are present in a person with depression. Negative automatic thoughts (NATS), underlying assumptions or rules (also called cognitive distortions that are described above) and core beliefs.

Core beliefs, also known as schemas are the third and deepest level of thinking. Beck categorised core beliefs into three types that he called the cognitive triad. This comprised distorted negative views of the self (e.g. I am ugly), current experience (e.g. Everything I do is a failure) and the future (e.g. I will never succeed in life). These negative core beliefs are formed by early childhood experiences and lie hidden in the unconscious until activated by life events. Once activated, these beliefs process information in a biased manner that further strengthen these beliefs and also refute or dismiss information that disconfirm these beliefs. For example, if your core belief of "everything I do is a failure" is activated by failure at an examination, you may discount the information that in the past you have passed many other examinations and focus only on the failure.

How do you change your core beliefs? Can they be changed at all? To understand this, let us look at how we are structured in cognitive terms. Cognitive structure consists of five elements. These are thoughts, feelings, behaviour, physiology, and environment. They interact with one another to create the prevailing mood state. For example, a person who fails an examination (environment) sees himself as an idiot (thought), becomes depressed (feeling), withdraws from friends (environment) and develops tiredness and lethargy (physiology). If you change any one of these elements, the other four would change. If the person who failed the examination decides to re-sit the examination (environment), he will see himself as being reasonably bright (thought), the depressed mood will lift (emotion), and he will feel active again (physiology).

In depression, cognitive therapy lifts the mood by changing a person's maladaptive thoughts. The first step is to identify such maladaptive thoughts. This is not easy as a person may experience a negative mood state immediately after a triggering event even without being aware of the maladaptive thought.

Maladaptive thoughts can be identified using different techniques. Maintaining a thought diary is one. Whenever a person feels a negative emotion, he is asked to write the thoughts that come to mind. For example, a person who feels low in the middle of a board meeting might think, "I am incompetent and my boss thinks I am an idiot." Once an adequate sample of thoughts of different situations over a period are gathered, the thought pattern can be analysed, and the underlying core assumptions understood. These thought patterns are then changed by repeatedly and logically questioning their validity.

Interpersonal Psychotherapy (IPT)

IPT is the second psychotherapy effective in the treatment of depression. It is an unusual therapy. Unlike other psychotherapies, it began as a manual for treating depression in a research trial.

In 1969 two psychiatrists Gerald Klerman and Eugene Paykel designed a study to test the relative efficacy of an antidepressant both with and without psychotherapy in depression. Gerald Klerman wrote a detailed manual of the psychotherapy to be used in the trial. The therapy was surprisingly effective and is now used to treat conditions other than depression.

IPT focuses on modifying disrupted interpersonal relationships or modifying expectations about those relationships. It is time limited and lasts 12 to 16 weeks. IPT is based on the attachment theory. Attachment theory postulates that human beings have an inborn tendency to form interpersonal relationships. The attachment style depends on the temperament and the environment. The particular environment style of a person is persistent across time and different relationships. Persons who are mentally healthy are able to form flexible attachments, develop secure attachments that are satisfying, adapt to stress, provide care to others when appropriate and receive care from others.

IPT focuses on primary attachment relationships and attachment styles. Symptoms resolve when patients repair disrupted relationships and learn new ways of communication to express their need for emotional support.

A metaphor for therapy
Sigiriya or the Lion Rock is situated in the Central Province of Sri Lanka. It is a massive rock outcrop 650 feet tall. It is a site of archaeological and historical importance and a UNESCO listed World Heritage Site. In 477 AD, Kashyapa, a king of Sri Lanka, built his palace on top of the rock. He also built a landscaped garden, one of the oldest in the world, and painted beautiful murals on the rock face.

The view from the top is breath taking. The climb, especially the last half, is along a narrow staircase built into the rock face. Not a climb for the faint hearted, but for the adventurous, it is a worthy challenge. For the majority, it is anxiety provoking and some self-talk that the effort is worthwhile is necessary to for the climb. Others need cognitive reassurance. They need reminding that many have climbed the rock successfully and not fallen off. This is a form of cognitive therapy. Others need more. They need a person to hold their hand and support them through the climb. Some are able to ask for this help directly and obtain such help successfully. A few, due to difficulties in their communication styles, are unable to express their needs directly or do so indirectly with whining and complaints, which reduces their chances of getting effective help. IPT is aimed at helping such people change their communicative styles so that they are able to effectively obtain help. Finally, there is a group of people who will never climb Sigiriya whatever help is given. Such people are beyond therapy.

Psychotherapy may look easy on paper, but in practice, it is not. Although there are several do-it-yourself psychotherapy books and even computer programs, for serious depression it is best to seek the help of a qualified therapist.

Chapter 4

Happiness

The word happiness, the entomological dictionary tells us, is derived from the Middle English word *hap* meaning *luck*. It originally meant "characterised by good luck" or "being fortunate". The meaning has changed over the years. The *Merriam-Webster dictionary* defines happiness as a state of well-being and contentment or as a pleasurable or satisfying experience.

Martin Seligman, a psychologist from the University of Pennsylvania, has written extensively on positive psychology. He says there are three kinds of happiness, and happiness is not a mere emotion or state, but a way of life.

The first is the pleasant life, which is trying to have as many pleasant emotions as you can and learning the skills to improve such experiences. This is the hedonistic cinema view of life where happiness is the diligent pursuit of and maximisation of pleasure. This view of life has not been viewed kindly by philosophers such as Seneca and Aristotle for whom the idea of pleasure was vulgar.

The second kind of happiness is called eudemonia, derived from the Greek. Etymologically, it consists of the words "*eu*" ("good") and "*daimōn*" ("spirit"). For Aristotle, it meant the 'good life' and the highest human good. There is, however, no consensus on what constitutes the good life or what sort of activities enables one to live the good life. For Seligman, a good life means understanding your strengths and changing the way you live your life to maximize those strengths. It means changing your work, your relationships, your parenting styles, your leisure activities to do the things you are best at. Another psychologist, Mihaly Csikszentmihalyi, has used the word 'flow' for this state.

The third kind of happiness Seligman talks about is 'meaning .' People may be in flow, but especially as they grow older, they look for this form of happiness – the pursuit of meaning. People who can attach themselves to something larger than themselves find more meaning in life than people who find meaning only in themselves.

In 1998, Martin Seligman became the President of the American Psychological Association. Each incoming president has to choose a theme for his or her term of office. He decided to make mental health or what made people meaningfully happy his theme. Mental health he thought should be more than the absence of mental illness. Just as a healthy person improves his physical fitness by diligent exercise it should be possible to improve mental fitness|. In other words, even people who do not have a mental illness can improve their mental health and live a more vibrant and happy life. Towards this end, he organised a conference in Mexico to which he invited the few researchers interested in human happiness. Since that conference and the subsequent promotion of Seligman's interest in human happiness, there has been a steady increase in the number of research papers and books published on the subject.

The determinants of happiness
The genetic contribution

Are we born happy or can we acquire a happy disposition? As mentioned in chapter 2, research has shown that 50% of a person's happiness level is due to a genetic set point. This genetic set point determines our general level of happiness. After a major stress or happy event we return to our baseline of happiness. This is similar to the set point for weight. Skinny people never put on weight whatever they eat whereas people on the heavy side have to keep to be careful of their diet.

Other contributions

What of the other 50%? The surprise finding is that only 10% of the variance in our happiness levels are determined by the differences in our life situations. Whether we are rich or poor, sick or healthy, good looking or plain, matter for only 10%. What makes up the balance 40%? It is our behaviour. We cannot change our genes, and life circumstance may be difficult to change, but if we could change our day to day behaviours, we could increase our happiness levels up to 40%. This is encouraging news. Let us look at how these behaviours could be changed.

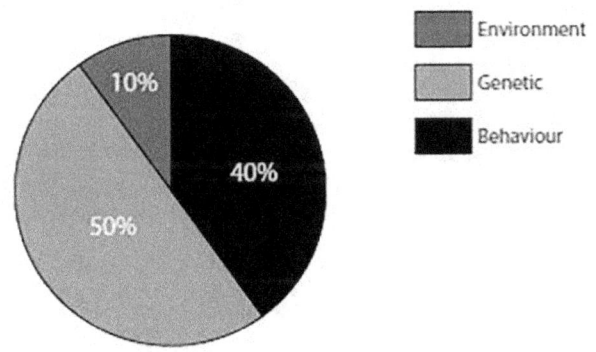

Fig. 2. Determinants of happiness

Edward Diener is the Smiley Emeritus Professor of Psychology in the University of Illinois. His nickname is Dr. Happiness. For the past three decades, he has studied human happiness. It is difficult to measure happiness. Even the happiest of people feel unhappy at times, and unhappy people have brief periods of happiness. In 1989, he created the Satisfaction With Life Scale (SWLS) (see next page). The SWLS is a short 5-item instrument designed to measure global cognitive judgments of satisfaction with one's life. The scale can be answered in a minute.

Satisfaction with Life Scale

Below are five statements that you may agree or disagree with. Using the 1 - 7 scale below, indicate your agreement with each item by placing the appropriate number on the line preceding that item. Please be open and honest in your responding.

    7 - Strongly agree
    6 - Agree
    5 - Slightly agree
    4 - Neither agree nor disagree
    3 - Slightly disagree
    2 - Disagree
    1 - Strongly disagree

- In most ways my life is close to my ideal.
- The conditions of my life are excellent.
- I am satisfied with my life.
- So far I have gotten the important things I want in life.
- If I could live my life over, I would change almost nothing.

Interpreting total score

    31 - 35 Extremely satisfied
    26 - 30 Satisfied
    21 - 25 Slightly satisfied
    20   Neutral
    15 - 19 Slightly dissatisfied
    10 - 14 Dissatisfied
    5 - 9 Extremely dissatisfied

In his book *Happiness–Unlocking the Mysteries of Psychological Wealth* written with his son Robert Biswas-Diener, he sums up the research findings on happiness. Their book state that happiness is not a place but a process. It is not simply a pleasant state that comes about by obtaining the good things of life such as health, a good marriage, and a large paycheck. Though it seems like common-sense, happiness does not come about by collecting the good things of life. It is more a process, a way of experiencing life that includes positive thinking, meaning, and spirituality.

The second major point they make is that happiness or psychological wealth is important for effective functioning. Critics have charged that as the emotion of happiness is transient, it is fundamentally an unrealistic emotion, the pursuit of which is a waste of time. However, research shows that this is not true. Positive emotions or happiness help people to be healthier, improve relationships, think more creatively, become interested in new activities and find work more meaningful.

"There is nothing either good or bad, but thinking makes it so," said Shakespeare in Hamlet, and the Stoic philosopher Epictetus said something similar, "People are not disturbed by things, but by the view, they take of them."

A happy mindset does help to keep a person happy and the Dieners in their book give useful advice on how we can maintain and foster a happy mind set. The acronym they use is AIM, which stands for attention, interpretation, and memory. Most people think that it is the interpretation that is important but forget that attention and memory are important too. To be successful at positive thinking you must first pay attention. I remember an old hymn I used to sing in school "Count your blessings, name them one by one.... See what God hath done.....you will keep singing as the days go by." So pay attention to your successes and blessings.

Is that a difficult task? Dan Simons is a psychologist. He is credited with creating a famous video illustrating the fallibility of human attention. For those interested, his video is available on YouTube. In this video, the viewers are asked to keep track of how many times a basketball is passed during a basketball exercise. At the end, the viewers are asked whether they saw anything unusual and most are shocked to be told that half through the video there was a man in a gorilla suit walking across the room. Usually when this video is shown to an unsuspecting audience, only around half notice the gorilla. The brains of people who are preoccupied with counting the passes block out the image of the gorilla.

The important lesson from this experiment is that our brains are not capable of taking in all the stimuli from the outside world. To cope it has to filter out some of the information. The problem is that in this process we might filter out useful information as well. The technical word for this phenomenon is inattentional blindness. This has implications for happiness as well. It has been shown that unhappy people tend to ruminate on their failings and flaws in character.

Professor Sonja Lyubomirsky migrated from Russia at the age of 10. She is now a psychologist at the University of California. She is also a leading researcher on happiness. She and her colleagues found that when people looked inwards or focussed on themselves they became less happy. Even happy people on inner reflection became less happy whereas if they focussed on outward things even unhappy people became happier. Of course, a certain amount of self-reflection is necessary but too much of it will drag you down.

Not noticing the good things around us is being like the people who did not notice the gorilla. There are always good, and bad things are happening in the world around us. Unhappy people will focus on the bad things and become unhappy. Happy people, on the other hand, look more at the good things of life. They will notice small acts of kindness in people around them or the beauty of nature like a glorious sunset.

The second letter of the acronym AIM stands for interpretation. Is the glass half full or half empty, is a question used to test whether one has a positive or negative view of life. The purpose of the question is to demonstrate that any situation could be seen in different ways depending on one's point of view or interpretation of the situation. How people interpret the world around them plays an important and significant role in how happy they are. People who interpret the world around them as difficult and hostile are likely to become unhappy, whereas people who see the world as a happy and friendly place are likely to be happy. Remember that song by Louis Armstrong,

"I see trees of green, red roses too, I see them bloom, for me and you, And I think to myself,
What a wonderful world."

Although interpretation determines the way we see the world, positive interpretation does not always lead to happiness. Sonja Lyubomirsky has more on the subject. She states that there are two other factors that are important: social comparison and retrospective judgment.

If you drive a Toyota car would you be happier if your

neighbour drove a Mercedes Benz or a Maruti? This is the phenomenon of social comparison. It describes that people compare themselves with others (neighbours, friends, family) when evaluating themselves and this, in turn, will affect mood. Poor people are more likely to be unhappy if they live among wealthy people rather than if everybody else around is also poor. An old Russian fable illustrates the point. Ivan and Boris were peasants, but Ivan had a goat and Boris did not. Then Boris found a magic lamp and the genie inside offered him one wish. Poor Boris could have asked the genie for anything in the world, but after thinking awhile Boris said, "I want Ivan's goat to die." Perhaps that explains why socialist revolutions are more likely in poor countries and led Winston Churchill to observe cynically, "Socialism is the equal distribution of poverty."

Research on the subject of social comparison is not always straightforward. Some people are inspired to do better by observing people doing well in life. A study in a cardiac rehabilitation program found that some subjects were inspired by others and did well in the program, but others felt downhearted and did not do well. Why do people think so differently?

Lyubomirsky studied how people felt when others in a competition fared better than them. She found that happy people were unaffected by social comparison. Regardless of the performance of others they felt good about themselves and enjoyed the game. In contrast, unhappy people became upset when other people were performed better at the game than them.

Lyubomirsky looked at how people make negative or positive judgments. We might think that our likes and dislikes depend on personal preference. But it is not so straightforward. A study of how students felt when they were accepted or rejected by a university, found that happy students tended to like the university that accepted them even more after receiving the letter of acceptance. In contrast, unhappy students still pined after the universities that had rejected them and were dissatisfied with the university that had accepted them. So it appears that naturally happy people reinterpret events so that their self-esteem is preserved.

What are the patterns of thinking that make people happy or unhappy? Albert Ellis a psychologist, and Aaron Beck a psychiatrist have identified patterns of irrational thinking that make people unhappy or even clinically depressed. We looked at their work in the chapter on depression.

The third letter in the acronym AIM stands for memory. Research has shown that we don't remember things exactly as they happen. Hyperthymestic syndrome-the continuous, automatic and perfect recollection of the minutiae of everyday life is a rare condition. In the book, *The Woman Who Can't Forget* the author Jill Price claims to be able to remember every detail of her life since the age of 14. But such super memory comes at a price. Imagine not being able to forget all the embarrassing and sad moments of your life! A little inaccuracy in memory is not a bad thing. It enables us to remember, with nostalgia, the good old days which perhaps were not so good after all.

This could be one way happy people differ from unhappy people. Maybe happy people remember happy events and forget the bad moments whereas unhappy ones do the opposite. Research shows this to be true. Happy individuals have similar negative and positive events in their life compared to unhappy persons, but they differ in how they recall these past events. People who are happy by disposition tend to err on the positive and view negative events in a more positive or humorous light.

Studies show that actively recalling good memories increase wellbeing. People who are asked to actively savour specific past events report feeling happier, compared to a control group. An important aspect of savouring is focussed attention. Spend some time each day thinking of your past happy memories and enjoying those positive moments and it will improve your sense of wellbeing. As Patience Strong once said, 'Your happy memories are like jewels in jewel box that you can take out from time to time and enjoy."

Increasing happiness
Here is Sonja Lyubomirsky's recipe for happiness, based on her work and that of others.

Count your blessings. You can maintain a gratitude diary where you write down once a week, three to five things for which you are grateful. These can range from ordinary things like good weather to more important events such your job promotion.

Practice acts of kindness. These can be systematic, such as giving a meal regularly to an old age home, or spontaneous, such as helping an elderly person cross the road. When you are kind to people, whether friends or strangers, it gives rise to a cascade of positive events, improving relationships all-round and causing people to reciprocate your kindness to you as well as to others.

Savour life's joys. Pay more attention to moments of happiness and joy.

Thank a mentor. If there is somebody out there who has helped you in important moments of your life, don't wait, thank him or her, preferably in person.

Learn to forgive. Write a letter of forgiveness to a person who has hurt you. Persistent rumination on past wrongs and thoughts of revenge has a detrimental effect on your mood. Forgiving increases positive feelings and gives you peace of mind.

Invest time and energy in friends and family. The most important factor in happiness is personal relationships, not money, job title or even health.

Take care of your body. Eat healthily, sleep well, exercise regularly and don't use addictive substances. A healthy body boosts happiness.

Develop strategies for coping with stress and difficult moments in life. Hard times come to all, but belief in a higher power or higher secular meaning in life has been shown to increase life satisfaction.

The downside of happiness

There are many books promising to make you happier. Numerous advertisements in the media offer counselling or therapy to make you happier. The politicians want you to be happier so that they will be voted back into power at the next elections. There is an industry touting various programs and treatments to make people happier.

Dr. Ed Diener disagrees. He says that he and his fellow researchers do not want you to be happier because you may be happy enough already. He contends that adding a bit of happiness to the lives of those who are chronically unhappy is a good thing but trying to make people who are generally happy happier may not be such good idea.

This is illustrated by an ill-fated experiment done in New York. A group of people decided that they could improve their level of happiness by agreeing to everything that was asked of them. At the end of a month, they were spent and exhausted, feeling very unhappy and angry towards all the people who had exploited them.

Is it good to score a ten on a 1-10 scale of happiness? The answer is probably not. In studies, the majority of people in prosperous nations scored between six and nine. Only a very few scored ten –extreme happiness. It appears that complaining a little is enjoyable and that perpetual happiness can lead to dullness and boredom. Imagine Jurassic Park without T-Rex. Would it not be a boring story?

Is there an ideal level of happiness? In bipolar illness (also called manic-depressive psychosis) affected individuals fluctuate between states of extreme happiness and deep despair. In the high or happy phase, these persons have elated mood, boundless energy and are able to work long hours without sleep. But this comes at a price. Such persons are also extremely irritable especially when their grandiose plans are thwarted, and they get little or no work done because their energy is without focus. They flit from

one grand plan to another with little accomplished. They get into social difficulties due to over spending and sexual excesses. Of course, this is an illness and not a normal state of extreme happiness, but it is a good illustration of

79

the consequences of an excess of a good thing.

In the Lewis Terman study mentioned in chapter two, the Termites were initially happy and gifted children. But later in life researchers found that the happiest of the Termites had died before the moderately happy ones. Perhaps the happiest were less cautious and took more risks like drinking too much or driving fast and, therefore, were more likely to die younger.

Happy people are more likely to work towards achieving their long-term goals. Are the extremely happy people able to achieve more than the simply happy people?

In a study done in 1976, several thousand college students were asked a single question about their level of happiness. Two decades later the study found that the students who rated themselves as happy were earning significantly more than those who reported they were unhappy. But surprisingly it was also found that the next to 'very happy' group was earning the most. So perhaps when it comes to happiness it is better to score an eight rather than a ten on a happiness scale of 0-10.

A group of scientists who studied the Leonardo da Vinci's famous painting Mona Lisa reported that she looked 83% happy, mixed with 17% of negative emotions. Perhaps that's the reason the painting is famous. A super happy Mona Lisa might not be considered a masterpiece.

Don't let scientists dictate to you what happiness should be. Happiness is an individual and private concept, and each of us has to work out our optimum levels and meaning of happiness.

Chapter 5

Influence- Obedience to Authority

On the 20th of January 1942 in Wannasee, a Berlin suburb, fifteen men of the Nazi hierarchy met in a villa near a lake. They were meeting to discuss a matter of great importance. All minutes of the meeting were destroyed, but one copy survived. The meeting was chaired by SS Director Reinhard Heydrich, a handsome psychopathic sycophant of Adolf Hitler. His task was to organise and obtain the cooperation of the top bureaucracy in Nazi Germany to carry out Hitler's Final Solution: a horrifying act that would ultimately lead to the death of six million Jews which would come to be known as the Holocaust.

How could a nation steeped in culture, a nation that produced the likes of Bach and Beethoven become a party to such an act of inhumanity? Is it that individuals of some nations are prone to obey authority to the extent of murdering people?

In 1961, the German war criminal Adolf Eichmann was brought to trial in Jerusalem reviving memories of the Holocaust. The question on people's minds during the trial was, "Could it be that Eichmann and his million accomplices in the Holocaust were just following orders or should we call them all accomplices?"

William Shirer the author of *The Rise and Fall of the Third Reich* thought that the Germans had an essential character flaw - a readiness to obey authority regardless of whether the request was outrageous or evil. Even if one man was evil enough to devise a plan to eliminate a whole race, it needed the cooperation of thousands of other people to implement. Stanley Milgram a psychologist at Harvard attempted to answer this question in a laboratory setting.

The Stanley Milgram experiment

The experiment began with subjects who answered an advertisement for volunteers for a study to investigate the effects of punishment on learning. A subject wired with electrodes was strapped to a chair. His task was to memorise correctly a list of words. Another person was asked to check whether the person remembered the word list correctly and punish him if he made a mistake. The punishment was supposed to be an electric shock. In fact, no electric shock was given, and the learner subject was an experimenter's helper who was asked to make deliberate mistakes. The real subject was the one administering the test and the 'shocks.'

The machine used by the person giving the shocks had an indicator showing that it could deliver electric shocks from 15 to 450 volts in increments of 15 volts. It was clearly marked 'mild' at 15 volts to 'danger-severe' at 450 volts. Every time the person in the chair made a mistake the person giving the shock was asked to increase the voltage by 15 volts. The person giving the shock was not told that the shocks were not real. The person receiving the shocks was trained to react appropriately each time he received a 'shock'. At 75 volts he would just grunt, at 100 he complained about the shock, at 150 he demanded to be released, at 285 volts he screamed and became silent.

The question was how far the person administering the shock would go before refusing to continue? Would there be any person who would go all the way or would all of them stop when the person being 'shocked' complained of pain? To the surprise and perhaps shock of Stanley Milgram, of the 40 subjects, 62% went all the way up to 450 volts.

Why did they do it? Unlike the soldiers guarding the concentration camps in Nazi Germany, they did not have an ideology to defend or their lives did not depend on obeying the researcher. What was surprising was that the behaviour was not specific to any specific submissive personality style but was present in the majority.

Milgram conducted more than one study. He carried out 18 variations of his study and was able to identify some of the factors that determined obedience.

The status of the location

The level of obedience was higher when the experiment was done in a prestigious setting such as the Yale University. When repeated in a rundown office, the level of cooperation dropped.

Legitimacy of the authority figure

People were more likely to obey orders if the person issuing them was seen as a legitimate authority with moral or legal backing.

Peer support

If a person had the social support of his friends in resisting orders the compliance was less. Also, the presence of people who were seen to resist the order reduced the level of obedience.

Personal responsibility

When there is less personal responsibility obedience increases. In Milgram's experiments when participants were able to instruct an assistant to press the switches that gave the shock, 95% (compared to 65% in the original study) went up to the maximum 450 volts.

Status of authority figure

When the experimenter wore a white lab coat the compliance rate was higher than when he was wearing casual street clothes.

Proximity of authority figure

It is easier to resist orders from an authority figure if they are not close by. When the experimenter instructed and prompted the teacher by telephone from another room, obedience fell to 20.5%. When the authority figure is close by obedience is more likely.

Stanley Milgram did not have to go to Germany to prove his point. There was nothing special about the German people that made them more vulnerable to authority. Even ordinary American citizens, who were neither sadistic nor brutish, were vulnerable to authority. The subjects who gave the shocks to Mr Wallace (the person who was shocked) did not enjoy it. They were nervous, fidgety and at times laughed nervously but yet they continued to give increasing levels of shock. To quote Milgram "...they are somehow engaged in something from which they cannot liberate themselves. They are locked into a structure, and they do not have the skills or inner resources to disengage themselves."

How did Milgram explain his findings? He postulated that people operated in two different modes. In the first mode, they operate in a state of autonomy where they have control over what they do. Under certain situations, people can switch into another state that Milgram called a "state of agency". To quote Milgram again, "I think of a state of agency as a real transformation of a person; a person has different properties when he's in that state, just as water can turn to ice under certain conditions of temperature, a person can move to the state of mind that I call agency. . .

the critical thing is that you see yourself as the instrument of the execution of another person's wishes. You do not see yourself as acting on your own. And there's a real transformation, a real change of properties of the person."

You might say that Milgram's conducted his experiments under laboratory conditions, and the situation was not very realistic. Would the same effects be observed in more ordinary circumstances?

Hofling Hospital Experiment
In 1966, psychiatrist Charles Hofling did a more realistic experiment on nurses. Twenty night nurses in a hospital received telephone calls (on separate occasions) from a Dr Smith (there was no such doctor in that hospital) who asked them to check whether there was a medicine called astroten (There was no such medicine and the bottle contained sugar pills) in the medicine cupboard. They confirmed that there was. The nurses were then asked to administer 20 mg (the maximum dose marked on the bottle was 10 mg) to a patient called Mr. Jones. Dr. Smith said he was in a hurry and assured the nurses that he will come as soon as possible to authorise the prescription. Of the 22 nurses in the study, 21 attempted to administer the medicine (they were stopped at the patient's door).

If the nurses did administer the medicine, they would have broken three hospital rules. First, they are not allowed to accept medicine orders over the phone from unknown doctors, second, the dose ordered was twice that of the recommended maximum daily dose and third, the medicine was not on the ward list of drugs. It was interesting to note that of a control group of 22 nurses 21 said they would not give a medicine ordered by an unknown doctor. It appears that we are not very good at predicting our own behaviour when under pressure.

The Stanford Prison Experiment

This study was conducted in 1971 in the Stanford University by the psychologist Phillip Zimbardo. It gives us a different perspective on how people behave when placed in a position of authority.

Zimbardo converted Stanford University basement to a mock prison. He advertised for students to play the role of guards and prisoners. Twenty four male college students were chosen and paid $15 a day. Participants were randomly assigned to the role of prisoner or guard. Students with a criminal background, psychological impairment or medical problems were excluded. With the cooperation of the Palo Alto police, the 'prisoners' were arrested at home and booked according to normal police procedure including mug shots and fingerprinting. They were then transported to their mock prison where they were strip- searched and given prison uniforms and a number.

The guards were also dressed for the part, with khaki shirts and pants, mirrored sunglasses to prevent eye contact and wooden batons. They were told that they could not harm the prisoners physically, but Zimbardo instructed them that, "You can create in the prisoners feelings of boredom, a sense of fear to some degree, you can create a notion of arbitrariness that their life is totally controlled by us, by the system, you, me, and they'll have no privacy... We're going to take away their individuality in various ways. In general what all this leads to is a sense of powerlessness. That is, in this situation, we'll have all the power, and they'll have none."

The first day of the experiment was uneventful, but after the second day the guards became increasingly abusive and the prisoners started showing signs of extreme stress and anxiety. More disturbingly, Zimbardo himself who acted as the prison warden lost sight of reality and allowed the abuse to continue. It was only when a graduate student Christina Maslach (whom Zimbardo was dating and subsequently married), voiced her concerns that he stopped the experiment after six days (the original planned length of the study was 14 days). Later Zimbardo was to write in his book, *The Lucifer Effect*, "Only a few people were able to resist the situational temptations to yield to power and dominance while maintaining some semblance of morality and decency; obviously I was not among that noble class."

What can we learn from this experiment? According to Zimbardo, it demonstrates the power of a situation in influencing human behaviour. When ordinary people were placed in a position of power, they started behaving in a manner they would normally not behave in their day to day life. The prisoners, in a situation they felt they could not control, became passive and helpless.

The study favours the situational attribution of behaviour rather than dispositional attribution. In other words, the situation, rather than our individual personalities, is responsible for our behaviour. It also demonstrated the impressionability and obedience of people when provided with a legitimizing ideology and social and institutional support.

In May 2004 shocking photographs of the physical and psychological torture of prisoners by theAmerican Military Police at the Abu Ghraib Prison in Iraq began to circulate. For Zimbardo, it brought back traumatic memories of his Stanford Prison Experiment and prompted him to write a book *The Lucifer Effect*, an attempt to understand why ordinary people do evil things. Zimbardo appeared as an expert witness for one of the accused MP prison guards.

However the accused received a harsh sentence and Zimbardo expressed frustration that the judge refused to consider that situational forces could influence individual behaviour. He was also disturbed that the senior officers, who because of their absentee leadership created the evil system, were let off scot-free.

Cognitive Dissonance

Leon Festinger was an American social psychologist best known for his theory of cognitive dissonance, a theory that teaches us important lessons on what influences our behaviour. A group of people called the Seekers, by Festinger, expressed the view that the world will end by a cataclysmic flood on December 21, 1955. Festinger reasoned that if Earth survived this date the Seekers would be in an uncomfortable situation. The Seekers were serious about their belief. Many members sold their possessions and quit their jobs. Some whose spouses did not share their beliefs, divorced. Their leader Mrs. Marion Keech believed she was a medium through whom extra-terrestrial beings from the planet Clarion communicated their wishes. Festinger was curious to see the effect on the group when nothing happened on the 21st of December. A member of his research team Stanley Schachter infiltrated the group and observed what happened. Did the group members give up on their beliefs and return home in embarrassment? Just at the right moment, Mrs. Keech received another message from Clarion stating that because of the groups' faith the cataclysm has been called off and the earth has been saved! The group dramatically increased their numbers in spite of the failed prophecy.

Festinger's cognitive dissonance theory states that we have an inner drive to hold all our attitudes and beliefs in harmony and avoid disharmony (or dissonance). Cognitive dissonance occurs when there is a conflict between our attitudes, beliefs or behaviours. The feeling of discomfort generated is called cognitive dissonance.

People try to reduce this distress by altering their attitudes, beliefs or behaviours. A classic example of cognitive dissonance is Aesop's fable of the 'Fox and the Grapes' which I am sure you all know. In this story, a fox sees some delicious looking grapes hanging on a vine. He jumps trying to reach them, but they are too high. He walks away comforting himself thinking "They probably taste sour anyway."

When a person is forced to do something that he does not want to do, a dissonance is created between his beliefs and behaviour (Festinger defined both beliefs and behaviours as cognitions). Forced compliance occurs when an individual performs an action that is inconsistent with his or her beliefs. The behaviour can't be changed since it is already done, so dissonance has to be reduced by changing his attitude regarding what he has done.

Festinger demonstrated this in a classic experiment in 1959. He asked a group of students to perform a series of boring tasks such as turning pegs a quarter turn over and over on a peg board. The students' attitude towards this was highly negative. They were then either paid one dollar or twenty dollars to tell another subject (an actor) that the task was very interesting. The students were then asked to evaluate how interesting the tasks were. Those who were paid only one dollar rated the task more interesting than those who were paid 20 dollars.

This was explained by Festinger as evidence for cognitive dissonance. The students experienced dissonance between the cognitions, "I told someone that the task was interesting", and "I actually found it boring." The students paid only one dollar were forced to internalize the attitude they were induced to express because they had no other justification. They had more dissonance than those who were paid 20 dollars, who had an obvious external justification for their behaviour, and thus experienced less dissonance.

A great deal of research has been conducted into cognitive dissonance. There have been some interesting as well as unexpected findings. It is a theory with broad application showing that we seek for consistency between attitudes and behaviours and we may not be quite rational in our way of reducing inconsistency or dissonance.

What is it important about these classic experiments by Milgram, Zimbardo, Festinger? The work of Milgram teaches us that we are all vulnerable to control by authority, and given the right circumstances, any one of us could be induced to carry out acts of harm towards our fellow human beings. The Stanford Prison Experiment of Zimbardo is a grim reminder of the insidious effect of power and authority. When people are placed in charge of human beings, their personalities undergo a radical change. It also reminds us of that saying of Lord Acton "Power tends to corrupt, and absolute power corrupts absolutely. Great men are almost always bad men."

Feininger's cognitive dissonance theory is applicable in our daily lives and shows us how we don't always think rationally and come to logical conclusions, and that our attitudes and behaviours are shaped by forces we are not quite aware of. A better understanding and knowledge of these factors would help us live happier and unprejudiced lives.

Chapter 6

Looking After Your Brain

In 1901, a fifty-one year old woman Auguste Deter was admitted to the Hospital for the Mentally Ill and Epileptics in Frankfurt, Germany. The attending physician was Dr Alois Alzheimer. He observed Auguste over the next five years. The patient initially was suspicious of her husband, and there was loss of memory. She forgot where she had placed things and lost her way even in her own home. She sometimes thought that people were coming to kill her. Finally, she died, bedridden and incontinent. Alzheimer autopsied her brain and using a special silver stain examined sections under the microscope. He identified the two hallmarks of Alzheimer's disease; waxy protein fragments called amyloid plaques, and twisted fibres called neurofibrillary tangles. In 1906, he presented the findings to the scientific community. The brain disease that he identified was named after him by a colleague Emil Kraepelin, a pioneer in psychiatry.

Alzheimer dementia

Today the 'A' word has come to be feared more than the 'C' word. Several prominent people like Iris Murdoch, Ronald Reagan, Charlton Heston and Margaret Thatcher have succumbed to the illness. What do we know about this illness more than a century after Alois Alzheimer described it?

The biggest risk factor for Alzheimer's disease (AD) is age. With an aging world population, the prevalence of AD has reached epidemic proportions. It is estimated that 40 million people worldwide suffer from the illness. It affects one in eight people aged 65 years and over and 45% of people aged over 85 years.

There is no definitive treatment for AD yet, but can we reduce the chances of getting it? Memory loss is the best known symptom of AD, but it is not the only one. There are other symptoms such as changes in personality and reduced ability to do complex tasks. There are several types of dementia but AD is the commonest.

There are also causes of brain injury other than dementia that lead to similar problems. Knowledge of such factors will help keep our brains functioning well in old age if we do live that long. First, let us look at factors that may lead to dementia or similar problems in later life.

Traumatic brain injury

"Float like a butterfly, sting like a bee" goes the song about Mohammed Ali, perhaps the greatest boxer ever. But years later he is a shuffling shadow of his former self. He has Parkinson's disease which, some doctors think, was brought on by the repeated blows he suffered to his head over the years. It has been known for some time that boxers are liable to develop a form of dementia known as dementia pugilistica, more commonly called the punch drunk syndrome.

Brain injuries are more common than we think. You don't have to be knocked unconscious to suffer a brain injury. Blows to the head can cause mild traumatic brain injury (MTBI) or concussion. These were thought to be not so serious, but now there is evidence that these are not trivial and can lead to prolonged impairment of the brain. This is more likely if there is repeated concussion (repetitive head injury – RHI).

Traumatic Brain Injury (TBI) is a leading cause of disability or even death in children and adolescents.

92

Those between the ages of 15 -24 who ride a bike, drive a motor vehicle or take part in contact sports, are at high risk of brain injury. Traffic accidents are the commonest cause, accounting for nearly half of TBI, followed by falls, assaults, suicide attempts and contact sports. TBI is significantly underdiagnosed and has no cure. Prevention is crucial, and helmets, seat belts, car seats and air bags reduce the risk.

Contact sports, especially in younger children are a significant risk factor for TBI. Mild concussions during sports are often taken lightly. The gender and age influence the outcome of head injury. In children under the age of ten years, girls are four times more likely to die than boys. It is thought that in boys the higher levels of testosterone make the brain bulkier and more resistant to injury. For young women, high levels of circulating oestrogen make them even more vulnerable to head injury. In older persons, this gender effect is reversed, and women over 50 are twice as likely to survive a head injury as men.

After a TBI, the cognitive functions return to apparent normality but subtle damage to an area of the brain known as the frontal cortex can have serious consequences later in life. The frontal cortex is damaged in 70% of children with brain injury. The frontal cortex controls emotions. Frontal regions of the brain grow throughout young adulthood. Blows to the head can damage the formation of insulation (myelin) around nerve cells which is essential for its normal functioning. This can impair ability to control emotions leading to outbursts of anger and inappropriate behaviour. Affected children can also have difficulty in planning complex tasks and responding to social cues.

In the year 2000, a consensus group of medical and athletic associations developed guidelines to help evaluate the seriousness of a child's concussion after a blow to the head during sports. The guidelines divide concussion into three grades.

In grade 1 concussion there is a short period of confusion, the child appears dazed without loss of consciousness. There may be inappropriate responses to easy questions. The symptoms disappear within 15 minutes. The child should be taken out of the game but if recovered after five minutes may be allowed to re-join the game. But if this happens twice in a one week period the child should wait one week before resuming any sports.

With a grade 2 concussion, the confusion can last from five minutes to an hour but there is no loss of consciousness. The child should be spoken to at five minutes intervals until the child appears normal again. The child should not re-join the game but stay away from sports for one week. If the symptoms do not disappear within a week, the child should be examined by a neurologist.

With grade 3 concussions, there is loss of consciousness atleast for a brief period. The child should be brought to hospital and subjected to a neurological examination. If the tests are normal and the period of unconsciousness was brief, the child could go home and resume sports in one week. If the results are normal, but the child was unconscious for more than a brief period the child should avoid sports for two weeks. If the nervous system examination is not normal, the child should have a CAT scan or MRI scan.

The type of sports most likely to cause concussion is boxing, soccer, rugby and hockey. You should take care if you or your children are taking part in these sports. Is there a connection between repeated head injury and development of dementia including Alzheimer's dementia in later life? A large study of risk factors for dementia known as the MIRAGE study found that patients with AD were ten times more likely to have a history of head injury resulting in loss of consciousness and three times more likely to have a history of head injury without loss of consciousness. Further research has supported this connection. So protecting yourself from head injury may prevent you from getting AD in later life.

Cell phones and the brain

For several years, there has been an ongoing debate about cell phone use and harm to the brain. In 2011, the International Agency for Research on Cancer (IARC) classified cell phone use as a possible carcinogen. In October 2012, Italy's Supreme Court upheld a lower court ruling that company director Innocenzo Marcolini's tumour in the left side of his brain was linked to his mobile phone use. He had used a cell phone for 5-6 hours a day for 12 years. He normally held the phone to his left ear with his left hand, while taking notes with his right hand. The evidence was based on studies conducted by Lennart Hardell, a cancer specialist at the University Hospital in Orebro in Sweden. The court said the research was independent and "Unlike some others, was not co-financed by the same companies that produce mobile telephones."

A large Danish study published in the British Medical Journal (BMJ) did not show an association between cell phone use and brain tumours. This study has been criticised because it considered only the length of a cell phone subscription and did not directly measure actual usage.

In April 2013, the *International Journal of Epidemiology* published a large prospective study. It was based on the

95

Million Women Oxford University Study in which middle aged women were asked about their cell phone use. The study did not show a definite link with any type of brain tumour. The authors point out that though cell phone use has grown enormously the rates of brain tumours in the UK have not shown an increase over the past two decades.

So where does all this leave the average cell phone user? Will another study in the future find out that there is a link between cell phone use and brain tumours? If there is such a link, the effect would be greatest in those who use their cell phones for long periods and hold them close their heads. The exposure to radiation could be easily reduced by cutting down cell phone usage time and using a hands free kit. It would be prudent to do so especially for younger people whose brains are still growing and, therefore, are more vulnerable to the effects of radiation.

Dementia

Let me now return to the topic that I started with, dementia. Dementia has many causes, and the chief one is Alzheimer's dementia. Many factors can cause or lead to activation of the disease. Let us look at the landmark research that led to the discovery of these factors.

The Nun Study

In 1986, David Snowden an epidemiologist started a remarkable study that lasted several decades. This is known as the Nun Study. Snowden at the time was a young researcher looking for a worthwhile study to secure his tenure with a university. He decided to study the effects of aging on a group of 678 Roman Catholic sisters, the school sisters of Notre Dame. This was an ideal group for an epidemiological study; the sisters did not smoke, used little or no alcohol, lived in a similar environment and did not engage in sexual activities. The sisters agreed to be interviewed extensively and donate their brains for research after their death. An account of the Nun Study is given in David Snowden's bestselling book *Aging with Grace*.

Each year the researchers returned to the convents to carry out tests and talk to the nuns. During one of these visits, Snowden came across a collection of biographies the sisters were required to write upon entering the order, some more than 50 years ago. He evaluated the essays based on the complexity of grammar and the average number of discrete ideas contained in every ten written words (idea density). He found that those who scored poorly on these two measures were much more likely to develop dementia. Sisters in the lower third sample were 60 times more likely to develop AD than a sister in the upper third.

Can we increase idea density in childhood? Idea density depends on at least two important learned skills, vocabulary and reading comprehension. The best way to increase these skills in children is to read to them and later get them to read a variety of books. We know that the brain is capable of growth and change throughout life, but most growth occurs during our younger years. Brain growth is strongly affected by experience and environment, therefore, we can reduce the risk of AD.

Snowden and his team also studied the emotions of the nuns and how this might influence their health and longevity. They studied the autobiographies for language style indicating positivity or negativity. Here are two examples, one from a 'positive nun' and the other from a not so positive nun. I am sure you can guess which one is which

"I was born on September 26, 1909, the eldest of seven

children, five girls, and two boys... My candidate year was spent in the Motherhouse, teaching chemistry and second year Latin at Notre Dame Institute. With God's grace, I intend to do my best for our Order, for the spread of religion and for my personal sanctification."

"God started my life off well by bestowing upon me a grace of inestimable value... The past year which I have spent as a candidate studying at Notre Dame College has been a very happy one. Now I look forward with eager joy to receiving the Holy Habit of Our Lady and to a life of union with Love Divine."

The study findings were remarkable. When the analysis was done nearly 60 years later, 42% of the nuns had died. By the age of 80 years, only 25% of the positive nuns had died whereas in the not so positive group 60% had died! Of the happy nuns, 54% reached the age of 90 while only 15% of the less happy nuns reached that age. Not only did the positive nuns live longer, they had healthier lives as well. We do indeed have a good reason to cultivate the habit of optimism and happiness.

As mentioned earlier, Alzheimer identified two primary lesions in the brain of his patient. They are called plaques and tangles. The tangles are found inside the nerve cell and appear as tadpole like structures in a microscopic slide when stained with a special silver stain. It consists of a protein called 'tau' which helps form rope like structures called microtubules. The microtubules are essential for communication between nerve cells. In AD the tau protein is abnormal and tangles the microtubules disrupting communication and ultimately the nerve cells die.

In 1991, German researchers Heiko and Eva Braak showed how the location of these cells can be used to stage AD. In stage 0 there are no tangles. From stages I through VI the number of tangles increase and spread through the thinking regions of the brain. The Braaks found tangles in the brains of persons as young as twenty. They proposed that changes of Alzheimer's disease start in adolescence and estimated that it would take fifty years or more to progress from stage I to stage V or VI.

The Nun Study did show that the number of tangles strongly correlated with the severity of dementia. However, there were exceptions. One sister who had died at the age of 85 had extensive plaques and tangles in her brain and was graded stage VI but had no signs of dementia when she died. Another sister who died at the age of 100 did not have any clinical or pathological evidence of AD and was Braak stage 0! Braak and his team found that 40% of the nuns who died between the ages of 96 and 100 were ranked as stages 0 or I. This indeed is good news. AD is not an inevitable consequence of aging, and there are other factors that if modified would allow us to escape the ravages of AD.

The Nun Study also shed light on how the second commonest cause of dementia known as vascular dementia (VaD) or multi-infarct dementia interacts with AD. In vascular dementia, the blood supply to the brain cells is reduced due to a series of small strokes or sometimes a large stroke which precede the small strokes. Any medical condition that predisposes a person to vascular problems such as high blood pressure (hypertension), diabetes or elevated cholesterol will increase the risk of developing VaD.

Previously it was thought that VaD and AD existed separately. Examination of brains of the nuns who had died showed that a third had a mixture of VaD and AD. It was also found that nuns who had the changes of AD in their brains were less likely to show signs of dementia if their brains were stroke free. It means that stroke free brains can compensate for the changes of AD and reduce the symptoms of the disease.

This is an important finding. We may not have a definite treatment for AD, but we know how to reduce the risk of strokes. High blood pressure or hypertension is the leading cause of stroke. Treating hypertension can significantly reduce the risk of stroke. Diabetes and increased cholesterol are other important risk factors for stroke. A diet rich in vegetables and fruits and low in fats combined with exercise and weight loss will control diabetes and reduce the risk of strokes. Smoking is another important cause of stroke. Giving up smoking will reduce the risk of dementia.

It is also important to know the symptoms of stroke. Numbness or weakness of one side of the body, difficulty in speaking, memory loss, dizziness or difficulty in walking and severe headache can be symptoms of stroke. If these resolve within a few hours it could be the result of a mini stroke or a TIA (transient ischaemic attack). It is important to seek medical advice as a TIA could be the precursor to a major stroke. Even in a major stroke, the first few hours are critical as the reduced blood supply to the brain lead to death of nerve cells and permanent disability unless the circulation is restored quickly.

The Nun Study helped lay some fears to rest. In the 1960s, a study reported that rabbits injected with aluminium salts had changes in their brains similar to Alzheimer's disease. Later it was shown that these changes were different to that of AD but by that time the supposed connection has been publicised by the media. The fear of aluminium toxicity made some people to throw out all the aluminium pots and pans in their kitchen. The research team in the Nun Study, after careful autopsy study, found no correlation between the amounts of aluminium in people's brains and AD.

People also worried that the silver amalgam used in dental fillings increased the risk of AD. It was speculated that silver amalgam which contained mercury released mercury vapour on chewing. The Nun Study team found no correlation between the number of dental fillings and cognitive test scores.

Diagnosing dementia

How do we diagnose AD? How early can it be detected? The classic bedside test is the Mini Mental State Examination (MMSE). It tests the ability to name specific objects, state the date, identify the location, spell WORLD backwards and other tasks. These evaluate components of mental function such as memory, concentration, and orientation to time, place and person. The MMSE is not very good at detecting early dementia. MOCA (Montreal Cognitive Assessment) is a more sensitive in detecting early dementia. The MOCA is copyright free and available on the web in several languages.

AD can be diagnosed definitely only after death. The brain is shrunken, and microscopic examination shows prominent collections of plaques and tangles. The concentration of these plaques and tangles increases with age and may be identified in those as young as 20 years. Until recently there was no reliable way of detecting these lesions in the living brain. A recently developed radio tracer called FDDNP binds to both amyloid and tau proteins. Using a PET scanner, the concentration of FDDNP in the living brain can quantify the amount of amyloid and tau. This indicates the risk developing AD. However, as shown in the Nuns Study, the correlation is not exact.

Treatment and prevention of dementia

Currently, we do not have any drugs or treatments to modify AD. The three main drugs in use, donepezil, rivastigmine and memantine are mainly symptomatic treatments. They slow down deterioration in memory for a period. For maximum effect, they should be started early and continued as long as there is benefit. Sudden withdrawal can worsen the patient's condition.

Gary Small is a Professor of Psychiatry and Director of the UCLA Longevity Centre. He has published over 400 scientific papers, and several popular books such the *Memory Bible* and *The Alzheimer Prevention Program* in which he summarises how we can reduce the risk of AD.

Even though we don't have medicines to cure AD we do know of ways of protecting the healthy brain. The lifestyle strategies keeps a brain healthy can be grouped under four categories. They are exercise, mental stimulation, reducing stress and diet.

Exercise

Several studies have shown the benefits of exercise for a healthy brain. Any form of exercise whether it is gardening, housework or sports reduce the risk of AD. Aerobic exercises such as walking, running or swimming are the best. Just twenty minutes of aerobic exercises a day improves memory and the improvement is maintained a year later even if the exercise is not regular. Although stretching and toning are important components of a fitness program, it has no direct benefit for improving brain function. Strength training such as lifting weights not only increases muscle mass and strength but also increases brain function and mass.

The hippocampus is a part of the brain that is important for memory and learning. It is also receptive to growth after physical exercise. It has been recently discovered that exercise stimulates the production of a protein called FNDC5 which is secreted into the blood stream. FNDC5 stimulates the production of another protein called Brain Derived Neurotropic Factor (BDNF) which in turn stimulates the growth of nerve cells and their connections (synapses). Regular endurance exercise strengthens and grows your brain, especially the areas concerned with memory and learning.

Another bonus of physical exercise is a reduction of depression, a condition that affects memory. Exercise also elevates the mood. A study done at Duke University found that exercise was as effective as the antidepressant sertraline in relieving depression. Exercise increases both endorphin and serotonin which are natural antidepressants in the brain.

Mental stimulation

Since 1948, the Framingham Heart Study has followed up 5000 people from the town of Framingham in Massachusetts. It was one of the first to show the relationship between hypertension, high cholesterol, and heart disease. It also showed a connection between the level of education and survival with good function. This could be due to many reasons and the association between good education and living longer with good function has not been clearly established.

The Nun Study found that the better educated nuns had a lower risk of death at every age. Those with a college degree not only had a better chance of surviving to old age, they were also more likely to maintain their independence and were less dependent on nursing care.

An important study published in *Neurology* by researchers at Rush University, Chicago reported that people over 55 years of age with a record of participating in reading, writing habits and other memory stimulating activities had 15% slower rates of cognitive decline.

Don't be discouraged if you don't have high educational achievements. Researchers have found that those with less educational achievements who engage in stimulating activities such as reading, writing, listening to lectures and doing crossword puzzles also performed well on cognitive tasks. Mental stimulation compensates for lack of formal education.

Reducing stress

Stress is known to cause cognitive impairment. It stimulates secretion of glucocorticoid hormones which appear to damage neurons particularly in the hippocampus, a part of the brain important for memory and learning. A recent study in rats found that stress hormones impair the functioning of the front part of the brain, known as the prefrontal cortex, an area important in high level executive functions of the brain such as decision making and working memory. Human studies show that chronic stress increases the risk for dementia and depression.

At present, there are no definitive studies which show that reducing stress reduces the risk of dementia. But early results are promising. Data from a study by Gary Small and others show that meditation can reduce inflammation and increase telomerase activity (telomerase is an enzyme that prevents the premature shortening of DNA strands when they divide, an important factor in aging).

Managing stress is good for your mental health. It may also reduce your risk of developing dementia.

Diet

Laboratory rats deprived of calories live significantly longer than obese rats. Living perpetually hungry is not a pleasant way of living a long and healthy life. People might prefer to enjoy their food and live a shorter life.

Hypertension and diabetes are important risk factors for strokes that in turn increase the risk of dementia. A diet that helps control these factors would help in reducing dementia.

Are there any special diets that reduce the risk of AD? The Mediterranean diet is a food regime inspired by the dietary patterns of people living in Greece and Southern Italy. It has a high proportion of olive oil, legumes, unrefined cereals, fruits, and vegetables, moderate to high proportion of fish, moderate consumption of dairy products, mostly as cheese and yogurt, moderate wine consumption and low consumption of meat and meat products. Olive oil is high in monounsaturated oils and fish has omega 3 fatty acids. They have been found to improve working memory and reduce the risk for mild cognitive impairment. Vegetables and fruits are rich in antioxidants known to improve cognition, and wine contains resveratrol a compound with anti-aging properties (at least in animals). Resveratrol is now available as a nutritional supplement, but its value in humans is yet to be proved.

What about other supplements that are supposedly good for your brain? The OPTIMA (Oxford Project to Investigate Memory and Aging) project was started in 1988 by Prof David Smith to study AD. The project studied both normal and cognitively impaired elderly persons until their death. This project examined if three B vitamins B1, B12, and folic acid given in high concentration slow cognitive impairment. Why would B vitamins help? These vitamins reduce the levels of homocysteine an amino acid. Patients with AD have unusually high blood levels of homocysteine leading to toxic effects on the brain. Early results from the trial showed that supplementation with these three vitamins improved cognition in a group of elderly persons. The most recent analysis from this project showed that when vitamin B supplements were given to people with high levels of homocysteine the rate of atrophy of the brain was reduced by as much as 90%.

The evidence for use of other supplements is not strong at present. A supplement that may help is cucurmin, an anti-inflammatory substance found in turmeric, which slows the formation of amyloid and tau in the brain. Parts of India, where turmeric in curry is consumed in large quantities, have lower rates of AD. Will increasing the amount of turmeric help prevent dementia? We do not have definite evidence yet. In the meantime enjoy your curry. It may be good for your brain.

Currently, we don't have a cure for AD but there is a lot you can do to keep your brain healthy and reduce the risk of dementia. The earlier you start, the better.

Chapter 7

Critical Thinking and Superstition

Superstition is a belief or practice for which there is no rational basis. The *Merriam-Webster Dictionary* defines it more precisely as "a belief or practice resulting from ignorance, fear of the unknown, trust in magic or chance, or a false conception of causation." The word superstition is derived from the Latin *superstitio* meaning super-stare, 'to stand over, stand upon; survive'. Its original intended sense is not clear. It could mean 'standing over a thing' in amazement, or the sense of excess in the performing of religious rites.

The *Encyclopaedia Britannica* classifies superstitions as religious, cultural or personal. Every religion has its own set of superstitions. A Christian opens the Bible at random and looks at the first text that strikes the eye and believes it will guide him in times of trouble. A Buddhist may offer a bodhi-pooja during stressful times. During times of trouble some ask an astrologer to read their horoscopes to find out whether they are under bad planetary influences. After the reading, the astrologer would recommend a bodhi-pooja or carry out other rituals to reduce the evil influences. People may light a specified number of coconut oil lamps around a Bodhi tree in a temple. Such religious superstitions are not a part of the core religion but built up around it over time. One person's religion, however, is another person's superstition. For the Christian emperor Constantine, non-Christian religious practices were superstition but, for the Roman historian, Tacitus Christianity was a 'pernicious' superstition. Many Protestant Christians consider the veneration of relics and images by Roman Catholics as superstition. For the atheist, all religious practices are superstition.

Cultural superstitions often intermingle with religious superstition. In Sri Lanka superstitious beliefs concerning methods of warding off ill, preventing accidents and sickness, bringing about good fortune, or predicting the future are ingrained in our culture. Other superstitions such as belief in the evil eye (*As waha*), and the wearing of amulets are not limited to Sri Lanka but are found in other parts of the world.

Personal superstitions are individual beliefs held by that particular person. For example, a person who gets good marks at an examination may believe that the pen he used is a lucky pen and will help him do well in examinations, in the future too. A businessman might believe that his business prospers because the business premises are 'lucky'.

Superstition has heavily influenced history and though we think that it is on the wane, in this modern age of scientific thinking where objective evidence is valued, it is not easy to let go our superstitions.

Today, even in an advanced country like the United States, more people believe in ESP (Extra Sensory Perception)

than in evolution, and there are 20 times as many astrologers as there are astronomers. Ronald Reagan when he was President consulted astrologers before scheduling international summits, presidential announcements, and even the flight schedules of Air Force One.

Astrology

Is astrology a science (as its proponents claim)? Can its claims be validated by scientific inquiry? A perceptive reader once wrote to the editor of a newspaper on the subject of science, "There are questions of faith, such as 'Does God exists?' There are questions of opinion, such as 'Who is the greatest baseball player of all time?' There are debatable questions, such as 'Should abortion be legal?', And then there are questions that can be answered to a degree of certainty by the application of the scientific method, which are called empirical questions, in other words, those that can be largely settled by the evidence."

If astrology is a science it too should be amenable to scientific inquiry. Has there been such scientific inquiry, and if so what has been the outcome? Hans Eysenck is perhaps the most famous psychologist of the last century. He left Germany in the 1930s and became the first Professor of Psychology in the Institute of Psychiatry, London. He is best known for his work on human personality. He also developed one of the most widely used personality questionnaires. To understand his research on astrology, it is useful to look at his work on personality. After analysing the answers given by several thousand people, he identified two fundamental dimensions of human personality namely, extroversion and neuroticism.

His Eysenck Personality Inventory (EPI) which contains statements that can be answered with a yes or a no was designed to measure these traits. People who score high on the extroversion scale are happy, optimistic, sociable and seek instant gratification. The introverts at the other end of this dimension are controlled and reserved, with few close friends. Most people fall in the middle between the two extremes.

The neuroticism dimension measures a person's emotional stability and those who score high have a low self-esteem, have unrealistic goals and often feel hostile and envious. Those who score low are more relaxed, able to face failure and can laugh at themselves.

According to astrology, six of the twelve signs of the zodiac: Aries, Gemini, Leo, Libra, Sagittarius, and Aquarius are associated with extraversion and six: Taurus, Cancer, Virgo, Scorpio, Capricorn, and Pisces, with introversion. Those in Taurus, Virgo and Capricorn are thought to be emotionally stable and practical and those in the three water signs, Cancer, Scorpio, and Pisces more neurotic.

In association with Jeff Mayo, a well-known astrologer Eysenck set out to find whether there was an actual association. Two thousand of Mayo's students and clients completed the Eysenck Personality Inventory. Skeptics expected that there would be no association between the sun signs of the participants and their personality profile on the Eysenck Personality Inventory. To the surprise of the skeptics and Eysenck there was a strong correlation.

The findings were hailed by the astrological community as "the most important development for astrology in this century."

Eysenck, however, wondered whether the strong belief in astrology of the participants had biased the study. People who were aware of the personality traits associated with their star signs may develop into persons with those traits or at least come to believe that they have those traits. Eysenck carried out two further studies to test his theory. In the first he studied a group of 1000 children who were unlikely to be believers in sun sign. This time there was no correlation between the children's personality profile on the EPI and their sun signs. In the second study with adults, he correlated their knowledge and belief in astrology with the correlation between sun signs and their EPI profiles. In those with knowledge and belief in astrology there was a correlation and in those without no correlation. The conclusion was clear; a person's sun sign had no relationship to his or her personality.

Those who believed in astrology countered by stating that the star signs were only a rough guide to one's personality and an accurate profile could only be obtained by studying the exact moment of a person's birth. This claim too has been refuted by the work of Geoffrey Dean a British researcher. If the above claim is true the personality of people born at the same moment and in the same place should be similar. He obtained the details of birth time from a database of 2000 persons born in London between March 3 and 9, 1958. Their exact times of birth and the results of intelligence tests and personality questionnaires administered at ages 11, 16 and 23 were available. From this database, he grouped people according to their time of birth (time twins as he called them) and compared their personality profiles. There was little similarity between the time twins.

In 1989, Verle Muhrer an American researcher published an article titled *Astrology on Death Row.* John Gacy was a serial killer who tortured and killed 33 young men and boys. Here was a person with a clear psychopathic personality. A researcher visited five well-known astrologers and gave each the birth time of Gacy and a birth chart (horoscope) cast by an astrologer of international repute. The researcher pretended they were his own and sought advice as to whether he should pursue a career working with young people. All five astrologers encouraged him to go ahead. One said that working with young people would "Bring out their best qualities." Another astrologer told the researcher that "He was kind, gentle, and considerate of others." A third astrologer told him "In the past, you have used your energies very well so, therefore, in this life, you have a lot to contribute, and your ... life will be very,

very positive."

The evidence suggests that astrologers cannot read a person's character from the position of the planets at the moment of birth, neither can they see into anyone's past nor predict their future. If the evidence is so overwhelming why do people still believe in astrology?

In 1948 American psychologist Bertram Forer did an experiment that would make him famous. He administered

a personality test to his students. A week later he gave the results to each of his students. Here is a sample:

You have a need for other people to like and admire you. You have a tendency to be critical of yourself. You have considerable unused capacity that you have not turned to your advantage. While you have some personality weaknesses, you are generally able to compensate for them. Disciplined and self-controlled on the outside, you tend to be worrisome and insecure on the outside. At times you have serious doubts as to whether you have made the right decision or done the right thing. You prefer a certain amount of change and variety and become dissatisfied when hemmed in by restrictions and limitations. You pride yourself as an independent thinker and do not accept other's statements without satisfactory proof. But you have found it unwise to be too frank in revealing yourself to others. At times you are extroverted, affable, and sociable, while at other times you are introverted, wary, and reserved. Some of your aspirations tend to be rather unrealistic.

I request you to read it yourself and judge how accurately it fits your personality. To his surprise 87% of Forer's students agreed with the description. He was surprised because the description he gave them was not their individual test profile, but a generic profile he had created from a newsstand astrology book. The conclusion: astrological predictions and horoscope readings need not be accurate. Give a reading that is general enough and give positive features to flatter sufficiently, and people will believe them. Psychologists call this effect the "Barnum Effect" after the great American showman PT Barnum

To quote the well-known skeptic James Randi, "From this and mountains of other evidence, it is apparent that, logically, astrology should not work. Couple this with the mathematical/physical fact that the gravitational influence of the physician's body as he assists childbirth has far greater effect on the baby being born than the entire gravitational field of the planet Mars."

Yet people continue to believe in astrology. As the great science fiction writer Isaac Asimov said, "It is sad that it does take courage, for trying to snatch folly from the minds of those who have been victimized by it is often rather like trying to snatch a bone from a dog. If human beings didn't find nonsense so attractive, there'd be no problem, for as someone said, 'Were there fewer fools, knaves would starve'."

Trance and possession states

'Do you believe in spirits?' is a question relatives of patients suffering from possession or trance states ask me. Usually, they are desperate because the usual rituals and ceremonies having failed to cure the patient.

Trance and possession states are commoner in Asian countries than in the West. Trance states are a detachment from ones' surroundings. In possession states, the personal identity is replaced by a new identity, attributed to the influence of a spirit, power, deity, or other person. They are associated with stereotyped involuntary movements and loss of memory (amnesia).

Possession states are seen in most societies. In a global survey in 252 societies, states of altered consciousness were attributed to possession. In most cultures possessing agents were thought to be spirits of deceased individuals, deities, animals, or devils. However, the identity depends on the culture.

Sri Lanka is home to the Theravada form of Buddhism. In its pure form, it is not a religion that endorses superstition. There is, however, a strong belief in the occult that pervades the culture. Its origins predate the arrival of Buddhism. There are two forms of healing ceremonies practiced in Sri Lanka, the Bali and the Thovil. In the Bali ceremony, the presiding deities of the planets (graha) are invoked and placated in order to ward off their evil influences. When a person is seriously ill the horoscope is consulted, and if the person is under a bad planetary influence, the astrologer might recommend a Bali ceremony. A Thovil ceremony is an exorcism to drive away malevolent spirits, known as yakshas, who are capable of bringing about pathological states of body and mind.

A trance deliberately induced as part of a ritual is not regarded as a disorder. If such states occur spontaneously or persist outside of the ritual practice, they are classified as a mental disorder. These disorders pose a problem for Western oriented psychiatric diagnostic systems such as the ICD-10 (International Classification of Diseases). In this classification trance disorder and possession states are categorised as a dissociative disorder.

In trance disorder, the individuals' attention narrows down to one or two aspects of the immediate environment. They lose a sense of personal identity. In possession states, individuals act out an identity different from their normal one. Individuals speak in a strange voice and take on the identity of the spirit that supposedly possesses them.

Dissociative disorders were originally called hysteria. The origin of the term is traditionally attributed to Hippocrates. Derived from the Greek word *hystera* for uterus, it was thought to occur only in females. The term was popularised by the French neurologist Jean Marie Charcot, who held public demonstrations showing him hypnotising hysterical patients. In the 1890s Freud wrote a series of articles on hysteria later compiled into his book *Studies on Hysteria*. Freud thought that hysterical symptoms protect the patient from mental stress (anxiety) or conflict.

Due to its pejorative connotations hysteria is now called dissociative disorder. Dissociative disorders are characterized by a disruption to the normal integration of consciousness, memory, identity, emotion, perception, body representation, motor control, and behaviour.

Several types of dissociative disorders are described depending on the affected function. The most dramatic is motor paralysis where an arm or leg is paralysed even though the nerves supplying the muscles are normal. In the sensory type, a part of the body becomes insensitive to pain. The loss of sensation is sufficiently complete for a needle to be inserted into the area without causing any pain. In dissociative amnesia, the person loses memory for a specific usually traumatic memory. In another type, the person forgets his or her identity and wanders away from home. In dissociative possession states, the person takes on the identity of another person usually a dead relative and speaks in that person's voice.

Dramatic though they may be, there is nothing magical

or supernatural about dissociative states. Psychological models explaining dissociative states have been described by Freud and others and have been successfully used in therapy. Freud postulated that hysteria was caused by the unconscious emotional conflicts, the resulting anxiety is reduced by conversion into a physical symptom. He called this the primary gain. Secondary gains are external advantage such as not having to work, which arise as a result of the symptoms.

Let me illustrate these theories with a few case examples. A school boy good in his studies was bullied at school. He did not want to tell his parents as he thought he would be called a sissy by his classmates. He suddenly became paralysed in both legs. This dissociative paralysis enabled him to resolve his conflict. Because his legs were paralysed he had a legitimate excuse not to attend school. He also did not need to tell the real reason for avoiding school. In another case, a young man on reading a letter from his girlfriend breaking off the relationship suddenly became blind. He could not remember what caused his blindness. A young woman who was mentally and physically abused by an alcoholic husband for years was possessed by the spirit of the husband's dead mother who severely warned the husband of dire consequences if he continued his abuse.

In all these cases, no magic was used in treatment. Simple psychotherapeutic techniques overcame the problems. In the case of the schoolboy, further questioning revealed the problem at school. After intervention by teachers and the parents the bullying stopped, the paralysis disappeared, and he went back to school. In the case of the young man who became blind, the treating psychiatrist was a competent hypnotist. A hypnotic trance state was induced, and the man taken back in time to the moment just before he became blind. He was suddenly able to see and remembered reading the letter from his girlfriend. He, of course, had to deal with the grief of losing his girlfriend. In the case of the possessed woman, you might well say that the possession is useful in preventing the husband from abusing her. However, it is likely that over time the husband would lose the fear of his dead mother's spirit and resume the abuse. A considerable amount of money had been spent on rituals to exorcize the spirit of the dead mother and the husband's alcohol problem was not addressed. A family meeting was held, and the woman was allowed to ventilate about the husband's abuse. She was taught better coping skills and the husband treated for his alcohol problems. The spirit of the dead mother went away at least for the time being.

Hippocrates (460 BC to 370BC) is the father of Western medicine. He taught that diseases were caused by natural causes and not by Gods or supernatural forces. His greatest contribution to medicine was to separate the discipline of medicine from religion. Yet more than two thousand years after his death people continue to attribute supernatural causes for disease. This is especially so for mental illness. Perhaps it is because there is a cause for most physical illnesses but, mental illnesses are identified by their symptoms and not by their cause. For example, tuberculosis is caused by an organism, that is visible under the microscope, but manic depressive psychosis, the mental illness is transmitted genetically and, therefore, has a definite physical cause, but since we do not as yet know the exact cause it is diagnosed by a characteristic cluster of symptoms.

Why should this be? As Hippocrates said, "Men think epilepsy divine, merely because they do not understand it. But if they called everything divine which they do not understand, why, there would be no end to divine things." People are likely to attribute supernatural causes to events or phenomena for which there is no scientific explanation. But again to quote Hippocrates, "We will one day understand what causes it (referring to epilepsy), and then cease to call it divine. And so it is with everything in the universe."

Isn't belief in astrology, horoscopes, spirit possession and its connected rituals harmless? Isn't it a part of the culture of a nation and hence to be respected and valued? I do not believe that it is harmless. Consider the large amount of time and money that is spent on these rituals with little benefit to the person. Consider the mental trauma that a person undergoes when given a dire prediction about the future that never happens. Consider all the problems that remain unresolved and the illnesses that are untreated because the patient or relatives are pursuing the occult. It is evident that such pursuits are extremely harmful.

James Randi is a Canadian-American, who started life as a stage magician and later became a scientific sceptic. After retiring at the age of 60, he used his skills as a magician to unmask psychics who use trickery to dupe their clients. In 1996, he set up the James Randi Educational Foundation (JREF). The JREF mission is to educate the public and the media on the dangers of accepting unproven claims of paranormal events or activities. It also supports claims into paranormal activity using controlled scientific experiments. The JREF administers the One Million Dollar Paranormal Challenge, which offers a prize of one million U.S. dollars to any person who demonstrates a supernatural or paranormal ability under agreed-upon scientific testing criteria. Though many have tried the prize is yet to be collected.

HL Mencken, an American journalist and critic who was also a critical thinker once said, "The most common of all follies is to believe passionately in the palpably not true, it is the chief occupation of mankind." Perhaps he was exaggerating but human beings have believed and continued to believe in what is palpably not true. Half of Americans still believe in creationism rather than natural selection in spite of overwhelming evidence for the latter. Many people still believe that the mind exists independently of the brain.

Critical thinking

Why is critical thinking important for mental health? It was a Polish monk Nicolaus Copernicus (1473-1543) who questioned what seemed obvious at the time that the Sun moved around the Earth. He died before his views could be seriously challenged, but others who shared his views fared worse. Galileo (1564-1642) was placed under house arrest for life, and Giordano Bruno was burned at the stake (1600).

Critical thinking may not make you popular, though you may not suffer the fate of Giordano. Knowing the truth has its advantages. It prevents people from wasting time and money with futile endeavours. If you have a depressive illness, it is far better to take effective treatment rather than do rituals and ineffective treatments. The depression might get better spontaneously, but it may also worsen and in the extreme, lead to suicide. Critical thinking may initially lead to the uncomfortable realisation of the true situation, but in the long term will lead to better solutions and more effective ways of dealing with problems. Ultimately it will lead to a less problematic way of living your life.

Scientific thinking is a form of critical thinking. The eminent scientist Carl Sagan wrote in his book the Demon Haunted World, "Science is an attempt, largely successful, to understand the world, to get a grip on things, to get hold of ourselves, to steer a safe course." He warns of what happens when we fail to think scientifically. "Avoidable human misery is more often caused not so much by stupidity as by ignorance, particularly our ignorance about ourselves." He points out that especially in times of scarcity and turmoil people fall back on primitive ways of thinking. He worried that "When fanaticism is bubbling up around us, then habits of thought familiar from ages past reach for the controls... Darkness gathers. The demons begin to stir."

Chapter 8

Existential Awareness and Death

Tomorrow, and tomorrow, and tomorrow, Creeps in this petty pace from day to day To the last syllable of recorded time,

And all our yesterdays have lighted fools, The way to dusty death. Out, out, brief candle. Life's but a walking shadow, a poor player, That struts and frets his hour upon the stage, And then is heard no more. It is a tale, Told by an idiot, full of sound and fury, Signifying nothing.

William Shakespeare, Macbeth 5.5 18-27

Macbeth's moment of existential crisis; it is part of one of Shakespeare's best known soliloquies. It is a wonderful formulation of death's inescapabilty and life as merely an empty preamble to its inexorable end. It is said that Macbeth was the favourite play of Abraham Lincoln and during the terrible days of the American Civil War, when thousands of men on either side died in battle, Lincoln often read these words from Macbeth.

An existential crisis is defined as a moment when a person questions the very foundations of his or her life and wonders whether it has any value or purpose. Two of the world's great religious leaders have had their moments of existential crisis.

When Siddartha Gauthama (later known as the Buddha), the founder of Buddhism was born, his father King Suddhodana was told his son would become either a great king or a great sage. The King wished the former for his only son and protected him from the poverty and sorrow outside the palace walls by preventing him from leaving the palace grounds. Despite his efforts, Prince Siddartha secretly left the palace with his charioteer to explore the world outside. During these journeys, he encountered an old man, a diseased man, a decaying corpse, and an ascetic. This experience led to an existential crisis, and he strove to overcome ageing, sickness, and death by living the life of an ascetic. Later, he abandoned this life and at the age of 35 attained enlightenment and was thereafter known as the Buddha (the enlightened one).

Jesus too had his moments of existential crises. The first was in the Judean desert when he was tempted by the devil. Some scholars including William Barclay think this was more a spiritual battle in his mind where he debated what sort of Messiah he was going to be. The second was in the garden of Gethsemane where he prayed for strength to complete his mission. Luke, in his Gospel, says that his agony was so intense that, "His sweat became like great drops of blood falling down upon the ground."

Existential psychotherapy

This is a form of therapy pioneered by the Emeritus Professor of Psychiatry, University of Stanford, Irwin Yalom. He does not claim that his insights are unique, but he is perhaps the first to use the philosophical insights on existentialism to develop a practical and coherent form of therapy.

Yalom says that there are four fundamental givens of existence that human beings worry about, either consciously or unconsciously. They are death, freedom and responsibility, aloneness and meaninglessness. I will first discuss the latter three fears and last, the most important fear, death.

Freedom and Responsibility

You may think it odd that freedom should cause anxiety. We normally view freedom as a positive concept, but in the existential sense, freedom means a lack of structure and design. With freedom comes responsibility. The sense that you are entirely responsible for your destiny can be a terrifying thought.

Psychiatry traditionally teaches that the time of greatest danger of a depressed patient committing suicide is not when they are severely depressed, but when they are recovering. When a person is severely depressed they lack the energy and the will, even to end their life. With partial recovery, some of the energy comes back but the mood is still depressed hence the increased danger. But I suspect that there is more to this. When people are severely depressed or suffering from any severe illness, the person is given freedom from social responsibility. This was called the Sick Role by the sociologist Talcott Parsons. With gradual recovery comes increasing responsibility, and this could be highly stressful especially for a depressed person.

A person I was treating recently for depression committed suicide. He was a medical student studying in another country and had returned home because of his illness. It was a severe depression but with intensive treatment including electroconvulsive therapy he was recovering well and planning to get back to his studies when without warning he killed himself. We can never know the exact reason as he did not express his intentions to anybody, nor did he leave a note, but I suspect it was fear of returning to studies that made him kill himself. Freedom from illness and the responsibility of day to day living can indeed be quite threatening. Sometimes it is sufficient to lead to suicide.

Aloneness or Isolation

The other given of existentialism is aloneness. This is easier to understand. We may have many friends, relatives and loved ones during life but, when we come into this world, and finally have to face illness and death, we do so utterly alone. Yalom describes three types of isolation a psychiatrist might encounter with their patients. They are interpersonal, intrapersonal and existential isolation.

Interpersonal isolation is loneliness and refers to physical isolation from other people. It may be due to geographical reasons, lack of social skills, personality traits or being uncomfortable with intimacy. It is also dependent on cultural factors such as the presence of extended family, institutions that foster social contacts such as temples, churches, and sports clubs or even shopping malls, markets and family doctors.

Intrapersonal isolation is more a psychological phenomenon. It is a process by which a part of one's mind is partitioned off. For Freud, isolation was a defence mechanism in obsessional neurosis where an unpleasant experience was stripped of its feelings and isolated from thinking. We see this in a condition called dissociative amnesia where a person's painful memories are wiped from his mind. Some therapists think that early adverse experiences lead a person to suppress and isolate large chunks of one's personality leading to complete dependence on others' opinions. Such individuals are extremely lonely, do not have personal opinions and cannot exist independent of others. Gestalt therapy pioneered by Fritz Perl aims to identify the isolated parts of one's self.

Existential isolation is more complex than interpersonal and intrapersonal isolation. It is there in all human beings, no matter how sociable or well integrated they may be. Existential isolation is perhaps only fully realised when faced with death. As stated by Heidegger, "Though one can go to his death for another, such dying can never signify that one can take the other's death away from him." We can die for a friend or a cause, we can die surrounded by family but each of us dies alone. Death is the ultimate isolation.

It is exciting to be in a foreign country, but when we are away from home for long we become homesick. We miss the familiarity of home. But the comfort and cosiness of home is also an illusion. We surround ourselves with familiar things, friends, family and material things that give us the illusion of security and comfort. On occasions, reality breaks through, and we are jolted from our complacency. This can occur at times of stress, illness or disaster but since this experience is within us rather than outside, an external stimulus is not essential.

How do we shield ourselves from this dread of isolation? Unconscious defence mechanisms can, of course, bury the anxiety from conscious experience. However, the defences have to work continuously to be successful. Yalom suggests that a more productive way would be to confront our isolation resolutely and then reach out to others, not in panic and desperation, but with love and understanding.

Meaninglessness

The third existential reality is meaninglessness. The Universe we know is a very large place. Earth is an insignificant planet in this vast cosmos, and individual human beings are even more insignificant, and what we do has little or no impact on an indifferent Universe. Therefore humans strive, each in their in own way, to give meaning to their lives.

Viktor Frankl, the Austrian neurologist and psychiatrist I mentioned in chapter two, describes life in a concentration camp from the perspective of a psychiatrist. After enduring the harsh experience and the loss of most of his family, he concluded that even in the most absurd, painful, and dehumanized situation, life has potential meaning and even suffering is meaningful.

He describes how the image of his wife who has been transferred to another concentration camp gave him meaning and the courage to stay alive. He writes, "... My mind clung to my wife's image, imagining it with an uncanny acuteness. I heard her answering me, saw her smile, her frank and encouraging look. Real or not, her look was then more luminous than the sun which was beginning to rise. A thought transfixed me: for the first time in my life I saw the truth as it is set into song by so many poets, proclaimed as the final wisdom by so many thinkers. The truth – that love is the ultimate and the highest goal to which Man can aspire. ......I understood how a man who has nothing left in this world still may know bliss, be it only for a brief moment, in the contemplation of his beloved. In a position of utter desolation, when Man cannot express himself in positive action, when his only achievement may consist in enduring his sufferings in the right way – an honourable way – in such a position Man can, through loving contemplation of the image he carries of his beloved, achieve fulfilment."

Victor Frankl pioneered logotherapy, a form of therapy which treats patients by helping them to find meaning in life. Frankl did not agree with Freud's homeostasis principle according to which the human organism, through the pleasure principle, strives to maintain an inner equilibrium. The pleasure principle is quite visible in early life, but with maturity is suppressed by the reality principle which requires delay or sublimation of gratification.

Frankl believed that the pleasure principle does not explain many central aspects of human life. The necessity for humans he said, "is not a tensionless state but rather a striving and struggling for some goal worthy of him. It is a constitutive characteristic of being human that it always points, and is directed, to something other than itself."

Frankl divided the meaning of life into three categories. The first category is what one accomplishes or gives to the world in terms of one's creations. The second is what one takes from the world in terms of encounters and experiences. The third is one's stand towards suffering, towards a fate that one cannot change. Frankl's suffering in a concentration camp lead him to search for meaning in human suffering. For himself, he found meaning in surviving, so that he could complete his work of creating a valuable therapy. He found comfort in a saying of Nietzsche's: "That which does not kill me, makes me stronger." Suffering is meaningful if it changes you for the better. Even if it leads ultimately to your death, Frankl believed that there is meaning in demonstrating to others, to God, and to oneself that one can suffer and die with dignity.

Freedom, isolation and lack of meaning are all important existential realities that make human beings depressed and anxious. However, the greatest and the most anxiety provoking of all is death.

Death

Death is the most obvious and most easily comprehended ultimate concern. We are here one day and are gone tomorrow, and there is no escape from it. Great thinkers, usually in the latter half of their lives, have written about it. If you think carefully, death does not simply follow life. In biology, the boundary between life and death is precise and finite but psychologically life and death blend into one another. As Montaigne said in his famous essay on death, "Why do you fear your last day? It contributes no more to your death than each of the others. The last step does not cause the fatigue, but reveals it." Death and life co-exist intermingled with one another and are interdependent. If we were to confront this fact, rather than causing great anxiety can it give us freedom from the fear of death? This is what existential psychotherapy aims to do.

Martin Heidegger, a German philosopher, was a pioneer of existential philosophy. He believed that there were two fundamental modes of existence in the world. They were: a state of forgetfulness of being and a state of mindfulness of being. Most of us spend the greater part of our time in the first state. We immerse ourselves in the day to day routine of life and worry about the way things are. When we enter the second mode of existence, the state of mindfulness of being, we marvel not at the way things are but that they are. For example, we may at times become annoyed at the behaviour of someone we love, the way things are, but in the state of mindfulness, we would simply be glad that they are there and be happy in their mere presence. Unfortunately, it is not easy to move from a state of forgetfulness to a state of mindfulness. There are certain urgent experiences that jolt us and shift our mode. One such important experience is having to face death.

There are two fundamental ways in which humans deal with the anxiety of death. In the first, we believe that somehow we are special beings and death will not touch us. True we know that someday we will die but that is in the distant future. When a person is told that he or she has a fatal illness, the first reaction is that of unbelief or denial. This is a defence mechanism, a psychological device to protect one's self from anxiety. Once this defence is breached, anxiety comes flooding in. Some may also feel angry or betrayed on discovering that their specialness is a myth. As Robert Frost said so beautifully, "Forgive O Lord my little joke on Thee/And I'll forgive Thy great big one on me." This feeling of specialness has its advantages in that it enables a person to face the dangers of everyday life and to strive for power and wealth and build great monuments.

The second fundamental manner by which man deals with anxiety is by his belief in a personal omnipotent being. Humankind, from the beginning of history, has believed in a personal god or gods. Some may find their God in an earthly leader or higher cause.

Confrontation with death though initially anxiety provoking can also lead to growth and change. A good example of such a change in the literature is that of Ebenezer Scrooge in Charles Dickens's Christmas Carol. The miser Scrooge is shown his own miserable death by a spirit and makes a radical change in his life.

Yalom has worked for many years in group therapy with patients terminally ill with cancer. Almost all his patients reported startling shifts in their view of life. These patients reported a sense of liberation, a rearrangement of life's priorities and a trivialising of the trivial. They had an enhanced sense of living in the immediate present rather than in the past and or postponing life until retirement.

They had a vivid appreciation of the simple things of life. They started communicating at a deeper level with loved ones and finally had fewer interpersonal fears with less concern about rejection and a greater willingness to take risks. Their only regret was that they had to wait till they were diagnosed with a terminal illness to make these changes.

Eternal life

It is the hope of all humans that when they die some part of them would continue on to eternity. The specific nature of such a belief would depend on the person's religion or belief system about afterlife. For the Christians, it is the resurrection and for the Buddhist it is rebirth. Science cannot prove an afterlife and currently, there is no proof that our mind or spirit exists outside of our brain.

There is strong evidence that all humans who live now originated from a tribe living in a part of Africa. If true, we all carry a portion of the genes of our first ancestors. In that sense, we are eternal or at least a little part of us would survive till the end of civilisation. Perhaps that is of little comfort to us as we would not have any conscious awareness of our existence.

Other than a belief in an afterlife, or denial is there a way in which we can relieve death anxiety? All human beings experience death anxiety, but some experience it more than others. It is an interesting and important research finding that death anxiety is inversely proportional to life satisfaction. We expect that people who are disillusioned and have led unsatisfied lives would welcome the idea of death, but the truth is the opposite. If we can find meaning in our lives and tap into the joys that life has to offer we might be able to face death if not with equanimity at least with less trepidation.

I end with the Epic of Gilgamesh, which illustrates the reluctance of humans, especially those who have achieved greatness to die.

Around 1100 B.C., a poet named Sîn-leqi-unninni wrote down this wonderful story just as Homer composed the Iliad. It tells the story of a historical King Gilgamesh who ruled the Mesopotamian city of Uruk. Gilgamesh was a king of great strength and beauty. Having accomplished many great deeds he did not want to die. So he set out to find a way to have eternal life. After facing many dangers and much suffering he came across a couple, Utnapishtim and his wife, who having survived a worldwide flood (this was before Noah!) have achieved immortality.

Gilgamesh narrates all the tribulations he has gone through and begs them to tell him the secret of eternal life. Utnapishtim takes pity on Gilgamesh and instructs him to dive near the shore of the Waters of Death to obtain a plant that will give him immortality. Gilgamesh does as instructed and obtains the plant, but before he eats it, he wants to bathe and purify himself. While bathing, a snake comes along and eats the plant. Gilgamesh now realises he has failed in his quest and that he would die. He returns to Uruk and accepts that, though he would die, his many accomplishments would bring happiness to his people, and his name and reputation would live on after his death.

In the end, Gilgamesh learns the same lesson as Achilles: What matters is what we achieve in this life, not how long we live.

Appendix - Literature

Chapter 1 - Stress and Coping with Stress
Atkinson & Hilgard's Introduction to Psychology: Susan Nolen-Hoeksema, Barbara L. Fredrickson, Geoff R. Loftus, Willem A. Wagenaar, 2009

The Relaxation Response: Herbert Benson, Miriam Z. Klipper, 2000

Beyond the Relaxation Response: Herbert Benson, 1985

Relaxation Revolution: The Science and Genetics of Mind Body Healing: Herbert Benson, William Proctor, 2011

Ascent of Man: Jacob Bronowski, 1973

Families and How To Survive Them: Robin Skynner, John Cleese, 1984

Life and How to Survive It: An Entertaining and Mind-Stretching Search for What Really Matters in Life: John Cleese, 1996

Adaptation to Life: George E. Vaillant, 1998

Mans' Search for Meaning: Victor Frankl, 2006

Chapter 2- Managing Your Emotions
Emotional Intelligence: Why It Can Matter More Than IQ: Daniel Goleman - 2005

The Longevity Project: Surprising Discoveries for Health and Long Life from the Landmark Eight-Decade Study:

Howard S. Friedman, Leslie R. Martin, 2012
Nicomachean Ethics: Aristotle, Terence Irwin, 1999

Chapter 3-Depression
The Anatomy of Melancholy: Robert Burton, 2001

The Essence of Rational Emotive Behaviour Therapy: A Comprehensive Approach to Treatment: Albert Ellis

Cognitive Therapy of Depression: Aaron T. Beck, A. John Rush, Brian F. Shaw, Gary Emery, 1987

Feeling Good: The New Mood Therapy: David Burns, 2008

Interpersonal Psychotherapy: A Clinician's Guide: Michael Robertson, Scott Stuart, 2003

Electroshock: Restoring the Mind: Max Fink, 1999

Chapter 4-Happiness
Flow: The Psychology of Optimal Experience: Mihaly Csikszentmihalyi, 2008

Learned Optimism: How to Change Your Mind and Your Life: Martin E. P. Seligman, 2006

Flourish: A Visionary New Understanding of Happiness and Well-being: Martin E. P. Seligman, 2012

Authentic Happiness: Using the New Positive Psychology to Realize Your Potential for Lasting Fulfilment: Martin E. P. Seligman, 2004

Happiness: Unlocking the Mysteries of Psychological

Wealth: Ed Diener, Robert Biswas-Diener, 2008

The How of Happiness: A New Approach to Getting the Life You Want: Sonja Lyubomirsky, 2008

The Myths of Happiness: What Should Make You Happy, but Doesn't, What Shouldn't Make You Happy, but Does: Sonja Lyubomirsky, 2014

The Woman Who Can't Forget: The Extraordinary Story of Living with the Most Remarkable Memory Known to Science--A Memoir: Jill Price, Bart Davis, 2008

Chapter 5-Obedience and Authority
The Rise and Fall of the Third Reich: William L. Shirer: 1960

Obedience to Authority: An Experimental View: Stanley Milgram, 2009

The Lucifer Effect: Understanding How Good People Turn Evil: Philip Zimbardo, 2008

When Prophecy Fails: Leon Festinger, Henry W. Riecken, Stanley Schachter, 2011

Cognitive Dissonance: 50 Years of a Classic Theory: Joel M. Cooper, 2007

Chapter 6-Looking After Your Brain
The Alzheimer's Prevention Program: Keep Your Brain Healthy for the Rest of Your Life: Gary Small, Gigi Vorgan, 2012)

The Memory Bible: An Innovative Strategy for Keeping Your Brain: Gary Small, 2003)

Aging with Grace: What the Nun Study Teaches Us About Leading Longer, Healthier, and More Meaningful Lives: David Snowdon, 2002

Chapter 7-Critical Thinking and Superstition
Astrology: Science or Superstition? H. J. Eysenck, Nias, 1982

Dimensions of Personality: Hans J. Eysenck, 1997

Flim-Flam! Psychics, ESP, Unicorns, and Other Delusions: James Randi, Isaac Asimov, 1982

The Demon-Haunted World: Science as a Candle in the Dark: Carl Sagan, Ann Druyan, 1997)

Chapter 8-Existential Awareness and Death
The Complete Works of Shakespeare: William Shakespeare, 2005

Man's Search for Meaning: Viktor E. Frankl, 1997

The Will to Meaning: Foundations and Applications of Logotherapy: Viktor E. Frankl, 1988

Man's Search for Ultimate Meaning: Viktor E. Frankl, 2000)

Existential Psychotherapy: Irvin D. Yalom, 1980

How to Stop Worrying and Start Living: Dale Carnegie, 1990

Bibliography

Aristotle & Irwin, T 1999, *Nicomachean Ethics,* Hackett Publishing Co.

Beck, A T, Rush, A J, Shaw, B F, Emery, G 1987, *Cognitive Therapy of Depression,* The Guilford Press.

Benson, H & Proctor, W 2011, *Relaxation Revolution: The Science and Genetics of Mind Body Healing,* Scribner.

Benson, H 1985, *Beyond the Relaxation Response,* Berkley.

Benson, H, Klipper, M Z 2000, *The Relaxation Response,* Harper Torch.

Bronowski, J 1973, *Ascent of Man,* Little,Brown & Co.

Burns, D 2008, *Feeling Good: The New Mood Therapy,* Harper.

Burton, R 2001, *The Anatomy of Melancholy,* New York Review Books Classics.

Carnegie, D 1990, *How to Stop Worrying and Start Living,* Pocket Books.

Cooper, J M 2007, *Cognitive Dissonance: 50 Years of a Classic Theory,* SAGE Publications Ltd.

Csikszentmihalyi, M 2008, *Flow: The psychology of optimal experience,* Harper Perennial Modern Classics.

Diener, E & Biswas-Diener, R 2008, *Happiness: unlocking the mysteries of psychological wealth,*

Wiley-Blackwell.

Ellis, A 1994, *The essence of rational emotive behaviour therapy: a comprehensive approach to treatment,* Albert Ellis Institute.

Eysenck, H J & Nias, D 1982, *Astrology: science or superstition?* Penguin Books Ltd.

Eysenck, H J 1997, *Dimensions of Personality,* Transaction Publishers.

Festinger, L Riecken, H W & Schachter, S 2011, *When prophecy fails,* Wilder Publications.

Fink, M 1999 *Electroshock: restoring the mind,* Oxford University Press.

Frankl, V E 1997, *Man's search for meaning,* Pocket Books.

Frankl, V E 1998, *The will to meaning: foundations and applications of logotherapy,* Plume.

Frankl, V E 2000, *Man's search for ultimate meaning,* Basic Books.

Friedman, H S & Martin, L R 2012, *The Longevity Project: Surprising Discoveries for Health and Long Life from the Landmark Eight-Decade Study,* Plume.

Goleman, D 2005, *Emotional intelligence: why it can matter more than IQ,* Bantam Books.

Lyubomirsky, S 2008, *The how of happiness: a new approach to getting the life you want,* Penguin Books.

Lyubomirsky, S 2014, *The myths of happiness: what should make you happy, but doesn't, what shouldn't make you happy, but does,* Penguin Books.

Milgram, S 2009, *Obedience to authority: an experimental view,* Harper Perennial Modern Classics.

Nolen-Hoeksema, S, Fredrickson, B L, Loftus G R, Wagenaar W A, 15th edition 2009, *Atkinson & Hilgard's introduction to psychology,* Wadsworth Pub Co.

Price, J & Davis, B 2008, *The woman who can't forget: the extraordinary story of living with the most remarkable memory known to science-a memoir,* Free Press.

Randi, J & Asimov, I 1982, *Flim-Flam! psychics, ESP, unicorns, and other delusions,* Prometheus Books.

Robertson, M & Stuart, S 2003, *Interpersonal Psychotherapy: A Clinician's Guide,* CRC Press.

Sagan, C & Druyan, A 1997, *The demon-haunted world: science as a candle in the dark,* Ballantine Books.

Seligman, M E P 2004, *Authentic happiness: using the new positive psychology to realize your potential for lasting fulfilment,* Atria Books.

Seligman, M E P 2006, *Learned optimism: how to change your mind and your life,* Vintage.

Seligman, M E P 2012, *Flourish: a visionary new understanding of happiness and well-being,* Atria Books.

Shakespeare, W 2005, *The complete works of Shakespeare,*

OUP, Oxford.

Shirer, W L 1960, *The rise and fall of the third Reich,* Simon & Schuster.

Skynner, R & Cleese, J 1984, *Families and how to survive them,* Oxford University Press.

Skynner, R & Cleese, J 1996, *Life and how to survive it: an entertaining and mind-stretching search for what really matters in life,* W. W. Norton & Company.

Small, G &Vorgan, G 2012, *The Alzheimer's prevention program: keep your brain healthy for the rest of your Life,* Workman Publishing Company.

Small, G 2003, *The memory Bible: an innovative strategy for keeping your brain young,* Hyperion.

Snowdon, D 2002, *Aging with grace: what the Nun Study teaches us about leading longer, healthier, and more meaningful lives,* Bantam.

Vaillant, G E 1998, *Adaptation to life,* Harvard University Press

Yalom, I D 1980, *Existential psychotherapy,* Basic Books

Zimbardo, P 2008, *The Lucifer effect: understanding how good people turn evil,* Random House.

Review Request

If you found this book useful I shall be grateful if you will post an honest review. This will help me to improve the book. If you like to leave a review please go to the review section of the book's Amazon page. You will see a button that says "Write a customer review" – click that and you are good to go.

Thank you for your support.

If you wish to contact the author:

Raveen Hanwella – raveenhanwella@yahoo.co.uk